IT'S NOT PERSONAL JUST POETRY

Barbara Love-Bussey

authorHOUSE®

AuthorHouse™
1663 Liberty Drive
Bloomington, IN 47403
www.authorhouse.com
Phone: 1 (800) 839-8640

© 2018 Barbara Love-Bussey. All rights reserved.

No part of this book may be reproduced, stored in a retrieval system, or transmitted by any means without the written permission of the author.

Published by AuthorHouse 02/13/2018

ISBN: 978-1-5462-2902-5 (sc)

Library of Congress Control Number: 2018901914

Print information available on the last page.

Any people depicted in stock imagery provided by Getty Images are models, and such images are being used for illustrative purposes only. Certain stock imagery © Getty Images.

This book is printed on acid-free paper.

Because of the dynamic nature of the Internet, any web addresses or links contained in this book may have changed since publication and may no longer be valid. The views expressed in this work are solely those of the author and do not necessarily reflect the views of the publisher, and the publisher hereby disclaims any responsibility for them.

I would like to thank everyone that supported me during this long journey to completing this book. I want to thank everyone for the love and support, and endless reading of my work. I want to thank everyone that encouraged me to pursue this. I would also like to thank everyone that gave me something to write about, real or made up lol. I would like to send a few very special thank you to some people who played a very instrumental role in this book coming out. Lucille Muller for giving me the opportunity to pursue this and building a friendship and sisterhood along the way. And to Carla Mc Allister, our bond was so easy, what started out as a working relationship, turned into a friendship that turned into a new part of the family, thank you for introducing me to Lu, because you believed in my ability to get her mom back on track, I was put in a position to do my book. And to Donna Bracaglia, I have so many reasons to be thankful to and for you. You and the big guy embraced me like a daughter and went way beyond for me and my family, when you did for yours you included me and I thank you so much for that, and for typing up all my poems allowing me to get the ball rolling. SIP Louis Bracaglia Sr and thank you for everything. And to La Mesha Sturdivant, thank you for running back and forth to the bank and post office getting my money orders and sending them off so that this could be possible. And to my husband and best friend, thank you for supporting me in everything I do. Your love is so amazing and unconditional, I love you more than I can express in words. And to my children Tanesha, Asia, Znyia and Zakee , thank you for being my reason for not giving up. I love you guys will all that I am. And to my wonderful grandchildren Makhyi, Sameerah, Meesiah, Mark, Alia, and McKenzie anything's possible if you want it bad enough. And to my parents, Raymond and Catherine Gibson, thank you for teaching me the important things in life, and thank you for always having my back and being there when I need you. I love you both past the moon. And to my brothers I love you always because I know your love is unconditional. And to my mother in law Corrine, thank you for being one of my biggest supporters throughout all of this ,I love you mom. And to my Aunt Amelia Sturdivant, thank you for loving and nurturing me like I was your own, you don't realize how much you mean to me, your home has been my home for so many years. I know when I come to you I'm safe.. And to my Aunt Jacqueline Pierce-Clayton thank you for teaching me how to fight, not physically, but emotionally, thank you for those lesson you taught me that you didn't know you were teaching, I learned from you by watching. Thank you for keeping your door open, and light on I love you. I would to have really loved to have mentioned you all by name, but won't, in fear I might leave someone out. And last, but certainly not least, Kathy Carr my writing mentor, thank you for keeping me off the cliff and encouraging me to push through I love you and thank you from my heart. Again, thank you to everyone that played a roll in me getting this done no matter how big or small.

Ps. I dedicate this book to the memory of my good friend Lesley Cyprian and Sister in law Kimberly Bussey-Marshall, after all the idea started with them.

Contents

Acknowledgement xi
Accepting me First 1
Addressing the issues 2
Am I Dreaming 4
Black and White 6
Black Rose 7
Blind Trust 8
Can I testify? 9
Can you believe that 10
Chasing the next high... 11
Chocolate crème caramel 12
Choosing not to decide 13
Couldn't decide to live or die 15
Couldn't decide to live or die 16
Crushed dreams 17
Cumming without you. 18
Dear daughters 19
Disappearing act... 21
Denying our present 22
Do you really know me? 24
Dying a thousand deaths 25
Eyes wide shut 26
Finding Forever... 27

Fix what's broken...	28
Forgive me momma	29
Fuck Cancer	30
Free	31
Growing in and out of love	33
Have you ever...	34
I can't stand the pain...	35
I couldn't catch my breathe	36
I dare not question god	38
I don't know me, when it comes to you...	39
I'm changing...	40
I Pass the test	41
I use to love someone	43
If I were you	44
I'll cry for the little boy while you cry for the little girl.	46
I'm lost with you	48
Inside out	49
It's a wrap	50
Its just comedy, right?	51
Just a little bit.	53
Just Cause	55
Justifiable homicide...	57
Killing me slowly	58
Let me complete me...	60
Let's save our love	61
Looking for love	63
Love me enough...	64
Love never the same	65
Me myself and I	66
Missing pieces	67
Miss us with the bullshit...	68
My gentle giant	69
My little secret	71

My pledge allegiance 72
My reflection of you 74
New Orleans unseen 76
Paused..78
Pick up games 79
Prisoner 24-7-365 81
Raped.. 82
Say it's worth saving 83
Secret garden..85
Securing our daughters childhood............................... 86
Sex, lies and secrets 88
So far away... 89
So High 90
Someday we'll be free... 92
Speechless 93
Starting fresh 94
Suicidal thoughts 96
Trapped inside 97
Truth be told.. 98
The biggest C in relationship....................................... 99
The mire image 101
The naked truth..103
The same addicts with different addictions...............104
The scenario 106
This is love 108
True luv 110
Twenty eight days 111
We got that love Jones... 113
What is love?.. 114
What's your position?... 115
When it hurt so bad, and feels so good. 116
When the cut is so deep, it never stops bleeding... 118
Who I am 119

Who are we? 120
Who's hurting me, is it you, or is it me............................122
Who knew? 125
Who's behind those eyes? 127
Who's Family? 130
When it hurt so bad, and feels so good............................131
Why do I need you to love me so bad? 133

Acknowledgement

I would like to thank everyone that supported me during this looooong journey to finishing this book. I want the thank each of you for the love support and the endless reading of my work. I want to thank each of you for encouraging me to pursue this. I would also like to thank everyone that gave me something to write about real or made up lol. I would like to send a few very special thank you to some people who played a very instrumental role in this book coming out. Lucille Muller for giving me the opportunity to pursue this. And to Carla Mc Allister for introducing me to Lu because she believed in the work I did. And to Donna Bracaglia I have so many reasons to be thankful. You embraced me like a daughter and went way beyond for me and my family. Thank you for typing up all my poems and making it possible for me to get the ball rolling. And to La Mesha Sturdivant thank you for running back and forth to the bank and post office getting my money orders and sending them off so that this could be possible. And to my husband and my best friend thank you for supporting me in everything I do. Your love is unconditional and I love you more than I can express in words. Thank you babe for always being here for me. And to my children Tanesha, Asia, Znyia and Zakee Bussey, thank you for being my encouragement. I love you guys will all that I am. And to my wonderful grandchildren Makhyi, Sameerah, Meesiah, Mark, Alia, and McKenzie anything's possible if you want it bad enough. Catherine and Raymond Gibson thank you for teaching me the important things in life, and thank you for always having my back and being there when I need you. I love you both past the moon. And to my brothers I love you always. I would really liked to have mentioned you all by names but that would have been to many. Again thank you to everybody that played a roll in me getting this done no matter how big or small.

Barbara Love-Bussey

Ps. I dedicate this book to the memory of my good friend Lesley Cyprian afterall it started as a joint venture. I finally done it girl…much love

Accepting me First

Don't take for granted what you don't want to lose.
And don't hold onto something or someone out of gratitude
Show yourself the love you want to give,
if you don't make it yours, you can't make it his.
Loving yourself is the most important part.
And giving is nothing if it's not coming from the heart.
When you love to hard there's so much to gain.
So much to lose, so much pain.
You can't, move on if you are living in the past.
Expecting it to be something that didn't even last.
How can we call it a future if it's looking so grim?
Maybe if we stop looking on the outside.
We will learn what we need to know.
We have to nurture ourselves so we can grow.
Instead of playing games with someone other than yourself.
Put your priorities in order and pack the bullshit on the shelf.
No one can love me better than I can love me.
I'm happy with who I've grown to be.

Addressing the issues

How do you fight being denied? You can't, but you bare the mark of its presence right in your face and inside you slowly die.
You don't think about what it is that can make a person disregard you that way, so you excuse it and to them it doesn't matter anymore.
Do the fights have to get physical before you realize how much you're hurting me without laying hands on me?
Damn, double jeopardy.
How could you not know, when my misery is what's making you happy and your literally feeding off me.
Must you take pleasures in that? Damn
What more must I give you before you realize that our love wasn't a fair exchange.
I loved you more than you loved me, but am I unhappy, only with myself?
Why must we keep trying to hold onto people that don't want to hold onto us?
Why can't I deny you of something the way you denied me?
Why is my returning the favor considering adultery, even if I was never physical?
Mentally you played with my mind.
You had me create love that was fit for a king for you, anit that shit funny?
Do you realize that you had me and lost me in the same breath or does it not matter?

Love lost was never love?
Should you feel sorry for me? Hell no!
Your love was a lesson learnt.
You can't love a person that can't love him or herself, the shit don't fit.
So ask yourself, well what is it that I have left?
Room to learn and love yourself more.
The saying is, "men can't live on bread alone."
And women weren't built to love for two but we do all time.
Where is the reward in that?
Who gets to take home the trophy?
Who'll bare the scars?
There isn't a winner in love.
The pain you give someone, someone else will give to you.
It's karma baby and I'm addressing the issues.

Am I Dreaming

"Am I dreaming", is it really me, it can't be me I'm smiling.
I don't know the last time I been here and I must say, I missed being here. Maybe it took exploring to get you were you need to be. I see myself differently now.
I don't see the yes woman that I
Became accustomed to.
I won't pretend anymore.
I'm not going to shut my eyes and hope that the problems go away.
I'm going to address it when it happens because my happiness is important to. Now that we've become friends again I see you in a whole new light.
I see the person I first fell in love with.
I know that things aren't back 110% but 95 anit bad.
I know now that to love is to forgive.
I loved you for 23 yrs, and I'm not willing to throw it away for 3 bad years.
We promised each other for better or worse, so here I am.
Baby you have loved me more than you hurt me, vice versa.
I don't want to play the blame game anymore, we're both the blame for different reasons.
You know why I love you so much.
Baby you took the time to find out how to love me, and I know I didn't make it easy, but you never gave up on me or us.
You taught me the difference in being tough and hard.

You taught me that it was ok to love again after my first heartbreak.
And you always seem to be around for a lot of my first times.
Am I dreaming or am I fallen in love all over again.
It can't be a dream I'm standing up.

Black and White

You blamed me for a crime I didn't commit.
But not because you believed I did it, but over some dumb shit.
You hate me because I'm not like you.
Who gave you the right to judge me, who?
I know a man that best describe you.
And if you think about it you know him too.
He's the man that killed all the Jews.
Yeah, your attitude is no different from his.
You messed with my only means to support my kids.
Oh, but don't worry we'll be all right.
I have no problems sleeping at night.
I have a question can you answer it please.
When you look in the mirror who do you see.
Do you see a reflection of your self, or a reflection of me?
Now ask yourself what does it all mean.
You purposely tried to destroy my dreams.
So before you start throwing accusation around.
Take the time out to find out what really went down.
Honey what you did was just not right.
But I understand it's
BLACK/WHITE

Black Rose

Hearts are breakable, friends are fake, love is questionable and lives at stake. Dreams become nightmares and lovers becomes foes. Relationships are questioned, while affairs are exposed. Families are being tested while kids are being molested. Cops become criminals while we're left with no protection. Gay is the new norm, while religions are being reformed. Street hustles becomes the highest paid profession, while teachers are being laid off kids are the ones suffering, is that the new lesson. What kind of world do we live in were religion is our biggest threat. When so many are overdosing and killing kids while on wet. Damn this is our life and we are not even in control. We are being lead like puppets, no bones, no souls. Chose to live or chose to die, nothing is giving but much is required. Who's getting over it ain't us, working 142 hours still making peanuts. Legally enslaved because we got a pay stub, easily replaced by the next sub. Its sad how easy it is for some to strip the beauty out of life. Taking it so easy not thinking twice. Changes are being made and things are out of control. To bad they don't see the beauty in life, even sadder they never experience the beauty of the black rose.

Blind Trust...

I give to much of myself to people that are not worthy of my time.
I protect people and theirs, I'm not sure if they will protect me and mine.
What do I have to do, to get you to understand ?
I'm more than who you think I am,
I'm gonna need you to stop acting like I'm some random chic you picked up off the street.
Either you do, or you don't want to mess with me.
You walk around with your chest out like you don't work for shit.
When in realty, you wanted it more than I wanted it.
Do you realize the type woman you dealing with.
I'm unpredictable and my mouth is real slick.
Friendship is the only reason you haven't been attacked with it.
Open your eyes, I'm more than what you see.
Stop looking at me like your looking thru me.
Stop being afraid, to let down your guard.
The role ur playing is tough, but not that hard.
Are you afraid that you might fall for me, or have u fallen already.
Have I given you something that has cause you to be unsteady.
Stop being afraid of me, I don't bite.
I don't want anything serious, just want a few nights.
If that's a problem don't worry I won't fuss.
After all we was fucking off blind trust...

Can I testify?

Can I tell my truth?
Can I give you my reason why halfway won't do?
Are you afraid that my truth may contradict your lies?
Why don't you want to be exposed, what do you have to hide?
It doesn't matter because I know who you are, and who you're not?
I know once a liar, always a liar, the cycle never stops.
What reason did you have to do me like this?
How can you love her and its me that you miss?
For the last year, all I get from you is lies.
Man up, stop living this lie.
Stop laying with her, and holding onto me.
Stop pretending what you have with her is real, when you know this is were you want to be.
I can't put my life on hold, until you decide I'm who you really want and need.
I can't save myself for you, when I feel I have to protect me.
I can't trust that look in your eyes, it doesn't match what you feel on the inside.
Damn, can I please testify?
Can I tell my truth?
Can I give my reason why halfway won't do?
Are you afraid my truth might contradict your lies, or tell the story, that's hiding in your eyes?

Can you believe that

I told him the way I should not see him in a week he better be dead. The week approached and I didn't see him, that Saturday he was dead.

Can you believe that?

I seen him on fathers day and I didn't stop to talk to him, that Wednesday he was dead.

Can you believe that?

I talked to her on Friday before mother's day and mother's day she was dead.

Can you believe that?

I never had the chance to tell them how much they meant to me and I was with them just about every day.

Can you believe that?

I took for granted that they would always be here.
I can't erase the fact that I didn't see him.
I can't erase the fact that I saw him but didn't stop to talk to him.
I can't erase the fact that I talked to her Friday and mother's day she was dead.

Can you believe that?

Chasing the next high...

Releasing myself from a mental jail that a twisted love affair caused. I was tricked and bamboozled into thinking that it was love. Your words was like mushrooms, it caused me to believe things was one way, when they were another. I was a quest that you had to conquer, and once you planted your victory flag I didn't matter any more. You didn't care that I was willing to risk everything, or that I did risk everything to be with you. The real issue is, you never loved me, you used me until you used me up and you dispose of me like dirty tissue. You shared this dream with me only to leave me out. No matter how hard I tried to get you to see I was who you needed, all you ever did was show me why you didn't want me. I can't began to understand how you can love me hard one minute, and disregard me the next. How can I go from being your everything to being your nothing. I have never experience so much hurt in all my years, but its ok, I'm gonna be just fine, although this isn't a clear picture of how it ended, let this be the story while we set out to chase the next high...

Chocolate crème caramel

As I approach the display counter I see it all laid out.
The white, the tan, and the coffee, and the chocolate crème caramel, the one that melts in your mouth.
I slowly run my hands across each piece I want to taste.
They all look so delicious, it's a shame a few will go to waste.
I'm real picky when it comes to caramel, just any piece won't do.
The piece I choose has to be soft, but hard, long but thick, bitter but sweet, and chocolate crème to.
I mean that's the best piece of caramel you're ever going to taste.
And believe me when I tell you not apiece will go to waste.
You pop that caramel in your mouth I swear you'll be in the zone.
And if you don't want anybody to know how you relax, you better take it home.
But if you're like me and don't care about the risk.
Unwrap that chocolate crème caramel and go for it.
Damn I like the sound it makes when it first hits your mouth.
The way it swishes around before it tries to pop out.
But you're quick and your tongue makes the save.
You slide it to the back of your mouth and softly suck until it deflates.
The more you suck and lick on it the smaller it becomes.
Once the liquid come oozing out that's when you know your chocolate crème caramel is done.

Choosing not to decide

As a woman and the strongest link of the family.
And considering the fact I wasn't built for this kind of struggle and yet I can honestly say I have the strength to keep carrying us.

But then I think, why should I, you've showed little interest or none, so why should I be the only one.
Give me a reason why you think it's worth it, share with me why you think I should keep fighting for this shit.

At least tell me your sorry and you never meant for me to get hurt.
Give me a reasons why you think this relationship will work.

As quiet as I sit, this is the whole scenario as I play it out in my head, it's a waste of time to bring it to you instead.

And with that and other things combined, shows me that you don't respect me and yet my feelings about us are confusing.

I can't help but think you don't respect as your wife or the mother of my kids, you don't respect for my accomplishments, my strength, and my determination to keep holding us together. You don't respect me for loving you unconditionally most of all, you don't respect me as a woman.

When I look in the mirror I don't see a reflection of me.

I see a reflection of some one unknown to me.
Some one I thought I'll never be.
The sparkle I use to have in my eyes is not there,
the smile is not there, the hope is not there,
thee enthusiasm, is not there.
Yet I keep choosing not to decide.

Couldn't decide to live or die

Look at the dope fiend standing on the corner trying to get her first trick.
Not because her kids are hungry, but because her body is sick.
She has to have that first bag to start off her day.
She has a monkey on her back that's driving her crazy.
Her body is trembling and her has are shaking.
And the fiend body is visibly aching.
She has a habit that's out of control.
A habit that will soon take its toll.
Now she has to ask herself is this the way I want to die.
Selling my body for a sleepy high.
Right now it's hard for the fiend to make the choice.
Without that bag the fiend has know voice.
Not once since she has been out there has she thought about her kids.
She doesn't know what they ate or what they did.
And right now she doesn't have time to care.
She got her first trick she almost there.
Now here's another one it's her second time around.
To bad she won't remember it because her body lies lifeless on the ground.
She took a shot to the back, and one to the head.
The fiend doesn't have to make the choice.
It was made for her instead.
I'm almost sure she would of chose to live.
Now that she is dead their hope for her kids.

Couldn't decide to live or die

(Part 2)

Sometimes it takes someone to die before you start to live and that's what I mean by hope for her kids.
Why couldn't she love her kids the same way or more than she loved her drugs.
Why was feeding her veins all she could think of.
Why couldn't she make the ultimate sacrifice when she was alive?
Why couldn't she do what she needed to do to survive?
Why must everything with her be a battle or war?
Why couldn't she just decide not to get high anymore?
I wonder what took place in her life that got her to this point.
Did she have dreams, what did she want?
Could she have prevented what she was going through?
I'm not sure what she felt.
She believed all she had was her self.
You know you get one chance to live.
Now her second has to be through her kids.
She couldn't decide to live or die.

Crushed dreams

Quiet, I can't think, I'm trying to concentrate, I have a lot on my mind.
I know you want to conversate, but right now is not a good time.
Okay, check this out, listen to this, it might sound crazy but this is some deep shit.
I've been dreaming of this man off an on for about ten years.
And today out of nowhere, the man from my dreams appears.
I was shocked you can even say stunned.
He's the man from dreams, he was the one.
I walked toward him never saying a word.
His mouth was moving but his words went unheard.
At that time I begin to challenge myself, trying to force myself to say something or even move.
Then he reached out and touched me sent chills down my spine.
My legs got weak, and my head got light, I thought I was losing my mind.
That's when it hit me, I've been loving this man for such a long time.
Dreaming of him often sometimes 2 times a night.
Girl guess what I did next, I turned and walked away like I didn't even care.
Girl I left the man of my dreams just standing there.
So can see why I'm a little fucked up in the game.
As long as I was standing there, I never got his name.
So since you want to talk tell me what that mean.
Me walking away from the man of my dreams.

Cumming without you...

As I lay here with nothing on but a pair panties,
I feel myself getting aroused.
I reach for the phone to call my friend.
I got machine, he wasn't in.
I can't wait this fire is starting to rise.
I'm moving as if I'm hypnotized.
As my mind start racing all over the place.
I'm starting to feel as if I'm trapped in a tiny space.
I feel like something has a hold on me.
My hips are swaying so seriously.
My eyes are rolling in the back of my head.
As my arms are reaching for the back of the bed.
My legs are now spreading apart.
And I can feel the surge of electricity and the intensity of the spark.
So I reached over and grabbed for the drawer.
And what did I find when I reached inside.
Mister Happy a personal friend of mine.
He took me places you wouldn't believe.
Places you'll only find while in ecstasy.
As I prepare to lay down and go to sleep, I realize my friend never responded to me.
Oh well his loss, not mine.
Truthfully speaking I'm doing just fine.
I tried my best to wait and let you do what you do.
Time was of an essences, so I had to cum without you.

Dear daughters

I'm writing this letter so that you can get the jist of what I'm saying. You ladies are beautiful as the days are long and I love each of you with all my heart and soul, know that I would give my life for each one of you. As my daughters you each play a very big part in my life. Tanesha you have few of my ways for instance you are a dreamer, you see good in everyone you'll give the shirt off your back if it puts a smile on someone else's face. You take on everybody problems like they're your problems their pain becomes your pain. And baby if I know nothing else about you I know that you love hard and you play for keeps. And your love for reading and writing just shows the passion you have for music just like me. Asia baby girl I see so much of me in you. Girl you are destine to do something your stubborn and you don't like to be told you can't do something. You are a fighter and protector. You protect even when the person isn't worthy. You also love hard and you wear your heart on your sleeve and you trust without thinking and it sometimes get you in trouble.

And the fact that your slick but not that slick mommy and daddy created that game (smile). Znyia I look at you and I smile baby I see so much of me in you. Ny you are a thinker you will dip your toe before you put your feet in. you don't like drama and you don't like to be in the company of people who do. And you will try your hand at anything at least once. You are not a selfish person you put everybody needs before your own. And the fact that you all look just like me shows how beautiful you are (smile).

And always remember that I love all the qualities that yawl have that you don't get from me. You girls have to promise that we will always talk and that you don't keep any secrets big or small. If you hurt I hurt. You cry I cry. Promise that you will always make time for each other please don't ever get to busy to be there for each other. And get in the habit of telling each other that you love them no matter how bad your moods are. I might not be able to give what you want but I promise to give you what you need. I will stand by you no matter but always be truthful. You young ladies are filled with so much talent you can be whatever you want to be and don't let anybody tell you different. Ladies, love is a beautiful thing but it's powerful, make sure whomever you give your heart to is worthy. Promise me that you will never put a man's needs before your own. Your dad always tell yawl, there's nothing they can do for you, that you can't do for yourself. And you know if you ever need us we will be there, nothing but death can keep us from it. And remember don't let anyone ever determine your worth. And don't ever do anything you can't look yourself in the mirror the next day. I'm not dying just wanted to remind you girls how much you mean to me.

Disappearing act...

What do you do when you feel you have no where else to go? When your only sunlight is darkness. When your pain run so deep your soul needs stitches. How do you cope, with not coping? How do reach when your arms stop in mid stride. What can I do to stop the pain, when pain is all you know. How can I love someone else when I hate myself. How is it that you stare yourself in the mirror, and not recognize who you are anymore? How do you convince yourself, your needed when you feel worthless. How do you fix a broken heart with ripped tape. What happens when the weight becomes to heavy to bare? How do you rebuild with crumbled bricks? What happens when you're to the point were you feel your better off dead than living. How do you fight for peace in a empty room. No matter how hard I try to stand I keep stumbling. I keep tripping over who I use to be. What happens when you stop appreciating you. I'm in a 3 alarm fire burning slow as hell and I don't even feel the heat. The truth is, I don't know who I am, nor do I know were I belong. As I stand here and look back at me, all I see is a shell of who I use to be.

Denying our present

Strange fruit hanging from the trees.
Blood dripping down the leaves.
For thirty years I've been trying to become head of the state.
Couldn't get on the ballot, had the wrong face.
I heard some say ain't no nigger gone run the white house.
Who the hell they thinks running it, what the hell they talking about.
The president politicking to put more money in his pocket.
Come on now, that fool needs to stop it.
Were fighting wars that has nothing to do with us.
He's asking us to support him but where's the trust.
He keep telling us to put on our bulletproof vest, he keep shooting us in the head.
One by one were dropping dead.
Democrat's shit ain't squeaky clean.
Their republican in disguise.
Once they get elected they change right before your eyes.
Vote for me they say I can make the economy better and create more jobs.
When in fact what their doing is political genocide.
Taking from the poor giving to rich this is some bullshit just plain sick.
Were fighting a war and making deals with the enemy and covering your tracks.
Baiting China, sending US citizen back.
Tell me again why were fighting in Iraq.

If you really want to fight a war find a cure for aids, meningitis, cancer and poverty or any other disease that we don't have a cure for.
Fight the war on racism and discrimination.
Fight all the inside separation.
Get your hands out my pocket don't you have enough.
Taking what little money I do make, making life tough.
Democrat, Republican what does that mean to me.
Not a damn thing, we have the wrong face, they don't see me.

Do you really know me?

Looking back to what got me to where I am right now doesn't seem so far off. I can actually remember times when I knew I should have been doing the right thing, but the wrong thing was better. I can honestly remember saying, I'll suffer the consequences later to whatever situation I was about to get into. And trust me when I tell you, whether you liked me or not didn't bother me, I didn't give a damn about you no way. But the funny thing is, we always seem to travel in the same circles, so what does that say about you. We still manage to end up in the same place, with the same problems. Thinking back, I didn't do so badly, I just did it different from everyone else. There's nothing wrong with being different, but it is something wrong when you think you're better than me. I see people looking me up and down trying to sum me up, thinking they done figured me out, because I'm in your presence doesn't mean you know me. I remember when I first found out I had big lips that tore me up. Here I was thinking because I was light skin I was perfect. I know people thought because I was rough around the edges that I wouldn't amount to anything, and here I am still here and confident as ever. And those same lips that yall thought was big are the same lips that have your asses in those seat listening to me speak. So tell me do you still think I won't amount to shit are you still sizing me up? Let me help you, you didn't know anything about me then, and you don't know shit about me now. I suffered the consequences and man knows I paid for my mistakes. I don't old anyone shit so stop assuming you know me and get to know me, that process is easier.

Dying a thousand deaths...

When I opened my heart to you I never thought it would be that last real conversation we would ever have. When I made love to you, I never thought that connection would be our last. It's crazy how what you want hurts you more than what you don't want. No matter how hard you try to pull away, it's like a magnetic force that keeps pulling you back. I can't put my hand on one certain thing that I don't like about you. I do know my feelings is like a mixed breed, Im not more one, than the other. I know when I inhale you, I exhale pain. It's not the familiar pain, it's pain with no description. I don't trust who I am when it comes to you. I don't know my place. I feel like everything becomes to big. My heart, my soul and my ego, all becomes to big. I feel there is no boundaries when it comes to you, and because of that alone, I'm dying a thousand deaths.

Eyes wide shut

Sometimes it's easier to forget than it is to remember. That's why it's hard to close your eyes, because you'll see all the roads you traveled good and bad.
What makes it even harder is that the things you try to forget are the things that end up haunting you. Who wants to remember being molested at a young age? Who wants to remember being judged at the age of twelve for making mistakes kids that age make. Who wants to remember their mother being beat for putting too much salt in the potatoes? Who want to remember that first heartbreak when you were in love and he just wanted bang you? The worse part about remembering is you can't forget. So it makes it much harder to move on. No matter how hard you try to do something good, the bad seems to out weigh it all. But what can you do when your eyes are wide shut.

Finding Forever...

How can you justify forever, if forever never came. How can you give more, when you feel less, and say nothings changed. It's over, there is nothing left to do. We can't paint this picture white, when all we feel is blue. I can't stand here and tell you I love you when I'm not sure how I feel. It's love, just not enough to keep me here. For the first time in my life I'm finally seeing people for who they really are. I'm not making excuses for the reason I have these scars. I tried so many times to keep this love a float. Your constant up and down, in and out, caused me so much hurt. You want me to walk around like things are so sweet. I'm walking on the bottom, while your standing on the top of my feet. You tried on many occasions to really break me down. You tried to force me to believe my reflection was what I saw on the ground. You planned for my downfall, all the while laying in my bed. You was never in my heart, but constantly in my head. It's ok I'm not broken, maybe a little bent. Only now I'm not stuck, or straddled across the fence. So please do whatever it is you have to do. Because from this point on, I'm done with you. Take my hand and hold it tight, once I let go your gone for life, I'm looking for forever, and your not it. I want better, I'm tired of the same bullshit.

Fix what's broken...

Is it over now, no matter what you do, good or bad, I can't feel it.
You have left scars in places, that love should have been the only thing touching.
You took something from me that I want back from you.
I wasn't a victim, I knew what you were capable of and I still stayed with you.
All I ever did was loved you from the moment we connected.
You made that same heart harden by the choices you selected.
How can the same hands that held me night after night, be the same hands that hurt me.
Why couldn't you just walk away and just let me be?
I loved you in the beginning because it was easy, now I love you because it's safe.
Now you stand before me and say you want to fix what's broken, shaking my head, the sad part about that is, you can't fix me.

Forgive me momma

I have tried to be the man you taught me to be.
I have tried to live by what you have instilled in me.
But mom somewhere down the line things got messed up.
I got confused and a little fed up, for whatever reasons, I wild out.
I took you through changes yet you stood by me when everyone else had doubts.
Mom I caused you so much heartache, pain and sleepless night.
I know I can't change that and man I wish I can.
But as a father now mom, I am a better man.
I'm teaching my boys the same values you taught me.
I'm trying to teach them the kind of man not to be.
I'm teaching them that a man is not self-made.
A man is not determined by the games he's played.
I'm teaching them the basic that makes a good man.
I'm teaching him that behind every good man is a great woman.
I'm teaching them that as a man he should be the strongest link in the chain.
At the same time respecting his woman and contribution she brings.
So mom please forgive me for the pain I caused.
And thank you for having my back through it all.
Mom I love you and because you're behind me I am a good man.
Forgive me mom if you can

Fuck Cancer ...

Cancer, I hate your existence because you bring so much pain.
You rip families apart, and cause such drastic change.
Cancer how could you be so freaking cold.
Preying on the body, and stripping it of its soul.
You cause havoc, on so many and you don't even care.
Taking lives, thats so not fair.
What's the reason they can't find a cure?
Or is it cancer's main focus to grip and destroy.
Cancer, I hate the very mention of your name, because of you, my family will never be the same.
Cancer you're the biggest legal terrorist I know.
Instead of shrinking, your attacks are on full throttle.
If I had to pick a weapon, I would say you're a bomb, because once you hit, all you leave is destruction behind.
Fuck you for the pain you cause, fuck you for no answer at all.

Overall, fuck you Cancer....

Free

It's so close I can taste it, it doesn't taste like victory it taste like freedom.
I'm learning to love the 2nd most important person in my life, me.
I'm learning the meaning of loving yourself first and then loving someone else.
And I must admit this is a wonderful place to be.
I don't know how to love me and you at the same time, and I don't feel like I'm taking too much of me from you, I feel like I'm taking what I need for me.
I don't feel guilty for wanting something for me.
I feel like I have a purpose, I feel like I can make a difference.
Why should a person like me who has so much to say keep her mouth shut?
Why can't I be the next Maya Angelou or Nikki Giovanni?
Why can't I hold their attention like Beyonce hold a note?
I'm just as capable as the one I compare myself to.
I belong in the race; I deserve to be here I've earned my spot.
I was temporally lost, but I'm back and all I have to say is watch out world because I'm coming through.
I'm not taking no for an answer.
And I'm not going to sit around and wait for it to happen, I'm going to make it happen.
I'm not going to allow anyone else to make decision about me, I'll make decisions for me.
I'll let you know what I can do.

I realized something I was expecting people to give me something I wasn't giving myself.
I was asking them to love me and I didn't love my self.
I was fighting for the wrong love I was dismissing the most important person.
Now I have rediscovered me I know can't anybody love me like I love me?
My love for me is unconditional.
I see my worth through me now not anyone else.
I'm better than all the bullshit I've been through.
And I don't regret any of it because I'm better woman because of it.
I know what it feels like to take a deep breathe with no hesitation, now I can tell you how it feels. FREE

Growing in and out of love

Three days and two nights of wondering were we going to be when you return.
Time is closing in on us and our fate sits two hours away.
I'm anxious because you promised me better things.
I'm scared because apart of me wants to believe it's going to be better, but I keep getting these bad vibes.
I know things will change, and some may stay the same.
Yet I'm not sure how to take it one-way or the other.
I've made myself dizzy trying to figure out how we are suppose to decide whose issues are more important, mines or yours.
When we first got together everything was perfect, we made choices together.
We talked about things before we done them.
There were times I fought myself to keep from fighting you.
Our lives changed over the years, but we keep telling ourselves it's just a growing experience.
Now it just feel different, you don't want the same things I want, and I don't want the same things you want.
Does that mean we don't want each other anymore?
Who are we kidding, we both know what it mean, we just can't bring ourselves to say goodbye?
If our love was meant to be, it will be, if not it wasn't for us.
No matter what happens between the two of us, know that I loved as hard as I could and I know that we didn't fall apart because we didn't love each other.
We fell apart because love was just enough to hold us together.

Have you ever...

I keep letting you back in each time I say your gone for good.
I keep holding on to you when letting you go seems so much easier to do.
What we share for each other isn't real, because if it was, it wouldn't feel so wrong.
We both keep moving on, to end up right back were we started from.
We are not teenagers anymore, its about more than me and you.
It's children involved are we prepared to keep hurting them with what we're putting them through.
Must we occupy space in each other lives when neither of us can acknowledge the other sitting there.
We only pretend to be over each other, and to us that's not fair.
Can you honestly look me in my eyes and say we are over for sure?
Can you look me in my eyes and say you don't love me no more?
I'm all over the place, because you ain't suppose to be here.
No matter how hard I try not to love you, I still hold you dear.
I always tried my damnedest, not to cause you any pain.
The more I tried to run from you, the harder you came.
I want to love you openly, but what we have isn't ours to share.
Help me find away to let go, help me not to care.
I don't want what we all most had, lets leave it in the past.
Chasing something we never really had.
Have you ever just loved someone, really, really bad.
Have you, Ever...

I can't stand the pain...

Love is a complicated emotion that we all experienced one time or another.
We put so much focus on one person that we lose ourselves in the struggle...
We get so caught up in the lies that seduced us, and the I love you, that fucks us into believing its real.

We trapped ourselves inside someone else, and pain is all we feel.
How did I love you when all the signs was there.
Not once did you say you loved me, but always said you cared.
Our friendship ended because it wasn't stronger than the affair.
A few dry fucks here and there...

Masturbation became a picture that was never frame.
Like a orgasm that never came.
A hill that couldn't be climb.
A situation that bottled the mind.
The release started coming at a rapid pace.
Letting go of you, to see the right face.
It's funny how things are no longer the same.
It's better now, I can't stand the pain.

I couldn't catch my breathe

I never gave credit were credit was due.
I took no part in the things we went through.
Especially since it's my fault that we're not together.
My scandalous ways was a tough storm to weather.
I made mistakes you wouldn't believe.
So what right do I have to ask you to put your trust in me?
Why should you want to work thing out.
When I was the one who chose a new route.
I didn't realize what I had at home.
I was in too deep to stop doing wrong.
But can you ever find it in your heart to accept my apology for hurting you the way I did?
Destroying your dreams of you and I having kids?
Erasing the fact that I was your lover.
Yet what should have been yours I was giving to others?
I can never give you back the (5) years in time, love & respect you gave me.
I can never give you back the patience, nurturing or stability.
I don't even know how to right this wrong.
I don't have a clue as to how to move on.
I know now I regret what I did.
I regret that you and I will never have kids.

I regret the fact that I put so much pain in your heart, and hurt in your eyes.
And I regret the fact I never tried.
Now that you're gone and I'm by myself.
I realized now it wasn't about any one else.
The night you woke up and got dressed and left.
That was the night I couldn't catch my breath.

I dare not question god

I played this scene over and over in my head and still I don't understand it.
But I dare not question god.
I want to know the reason for you leaving.
The pieces to the puzzle don't fit.
But I dare not question god.
I might not know the reason for him taking you, but I dare not question god.
I do know you're better off than I am today.
Yet, I dare not question god.
You had your whole life ahead of you.
You had only just begun.
But I dare not question god.
Yet he picked you, you were the chosen one.
But I dare not question god.
Father as your daughter you know I'm not without sin.
I've been sitting around racking my brain till I finally gave in.
I stood up sucked in my breathe and started forming words in my mouth.
The more I tried to roll them the words just wouldn't come out.
That was because I thought about questioning god.
God does everything for a reason so who are we to question god.

In memory of Lesley Cyprian

I don't know me, when it comes to you...

I find myself moving like a thief when it comes to you. I feel like I'm stealing from me, to give to you. I look around to make sure no one is looking then I give you a piece of my heart. Only for you to misplace it, and pretend someone else has it. No matter how many times I tell you it belongs to you, you show me reasons why it shouldn't, you never valued my heart. I find myself hiding, because I don't want anyone to know what I'm capable of taking from me, to give to you. I'm surrounded by so many beautiful possession but for the life of me I can't see them. Does the value go down when it's in the hands of someone that doesn't appreciate what I took from me, to give to you. I don't know my value anymore, but I do know, I don't like who I am when I'm with you...

I'm changing...

I'm changing right in front of you and you don't even see the change.
Same DNA, same height and weight, still the same name.
I have the same face with a brighter smile.
A lot more joy in my eyes.
I'm still me, just wiser now.
And I'm not letting anything bring me down.
I'm changing, I'm not the same.
I'm no longer consumed by pain.
I'm so much stronger than I use to be.
I'm no longer passive or naive.
I'm changing, do you see me?

I Pass the test

Why do you keep quizzing me like I'm a student in your class?
Like I have something to prove to you, when you're a mistake from my past.
I gave you a chance and you ruined it and I refuse to go backwards.
So you are just going to have to deal with whatever situation that occurred.
I don't invest time in sinking ships.
If we were meant to be, we would still be in a relationship.
Don't interfere in what I got going on.
You made the decision to be gone.
I can't look back on a couple years.
I got twenty or more years invested in here.
I found a man that has my back.
He didn't run when things fell off track.
He doesn't run for whatever reason.
He doesn't love me in certain season.
He' s here all the time, he doesn't constantly let me down.
He was here when you couldn't be found.
Now you trying to come around.
I don't owe you anything, and not asking for anything either.
I didn't need you then, I don't need you now neither.
Do you know what it's like to love someone and find out they don't love you back.
It's like a crack head trying to smoke soap when it appears to look like crack.

So again tell me why you trying to holla at me now.
Well your answer doesn't matter, I don't want you around.
So if you love me like you say you do.
You would walk away and forget I know you.

Pass the test.

I use to love someone

From the beginning, I knew I loved you.
I could never stop thinking of you.
Wherever you were, I wanted to be.
And even if we weren't together, you was always with me.
I would have never guessed, you'd be the one to pull me in and string me along.
You promised me forever, and took it back.
You hit the bumps while I swerve the cracks.
You took something you can't give back; it's elementary now because it's beyond the fact
You bet against us, not even given it a second thought.
You sacrificed more than just my heart.
Do you realize the pain is real?
You have know clue as to how I feel.
I rather give birth everyday, than to ever feel pain this way.
Suicide came to mind, as a passing thought caught in time.
I can't control my emotions cause their allover the place.
You forced me to see you and your other face.
Time and time again those thought comes to mind.
The harder I try to conceal them, the easier they are to find.
It's hard to mend a broken heart.
When the rest of you is falling apart.
As hard as I pray for this pain to go away.
I wake up relieving it everyday.
I can't remember once you saying I wasn't the one.
I remember now, that I use to love someone.

If I were you

To many times I stumble upon the truth about us.
Each time I confront you it turns into issue about trust.
How do you expect me to understand how you feel?
When every word that comes out your mouth is a lie, yet you talk about keeping it real
Time is running out and it's a lot at stake.
When are you going to grow up and step up to the plate?
I'm tired of your superficial understandings of how I am.
When the true reality of it all is that you don't give a damn.
The problem is, as I see it all, you want more than you can offer me.
You want me to be able to give you my every thing, and you don't carry any of the responsibility.
You keep deciding for the both of us.
You keep pushing me as if hurting me wasn't enough.
See, I thought foolishly from the beginning believing you loved me more than life itself.
When in fact you didn't love me, you loved someone else.
I wasn't faking when I was there when your back was up against the wall.
I wasn't faking when I told you I would be there whenever you called.
I wasn't faking each time I picked you up when everyone else that claimed to love you failed.
Yet you keep giving me love on sale instead of giving it to me retail

Damn I can't believe I let you do this to me again.
Only this time I know and still I wanted you as my friend.
But most of all I let you strip me of everything except my skin
My eyes, my jaws, my heart, my soul…all sunk in.
I never once pretended with you.
I was there for everything you've been through.
You just couldn't love me.
You just couldn't remain true.
But I would of loved to have someone to love like me one that loves honestly and completely.
Some one that's not afraid to love and be true to them self.
Some one to love me and no one else.
You act as if I broke your heart.
When you were playing with mine from the very start
I did every thing that you insisted
But my love constantly resisted
So there is nothing else I could do
I would have loved me, "if I were you"

I'll cry for the little boy while you cry for the little girl.

You asked, "who will cry for the little boy that cries inside of you," I will.
I know what it's like to feel alone when surrounded by so many yet so few far and between.
I remember what it's like to be standing in someone's presence, and still be ignored as if I wasn't there, looked at and still not be seen.
I know what it's like to feel full when you're really hungry and your stomach is against your back and your ribs feel like a knife jabbing into your skin.
I see those scars every time I close my eyes and ask myself how am I suppose to deal with that, how do I cover the scars that's left within.
Adults touching you in ways they should never touch a child, trying to comfort you by rubbing your back with that mischievous smile.
Wanting you to believe that they're not doing anything wrong, but always trying to find reasons to get you alone.
I'll cry for the little boy, while you cry for the little girl that cries inside of me.
The one who can't contain herself because like you she's angry.
I'll cry for you because I know what it's like to have your screams fall on deaf ears.
Going through the same shit day after day and year after year.

I'll cry for the little boy, while you cry for the little girl that cries inside of me.

Losing myself to find myself to only feel incomplete.

Like you I love someone to no existence at all, until real love walked in and I know longer felt enthralled.

I felt free for the first time like a newborn child taking its first breathe, me, like you had finally found herself.

So I'll cry for the little girl that cries inside of me.

I'm lost with you

I've been thinking about me lately, asking myself what is it that I want and this is what I came up with.
On occasions, I want to smile, I want to be looked at like I'm adored.
I want my man to hold my hand when I fell like I can't take it any more.
I want to be respected for my determination to live and let live.
When I give and not really have it to give.
I want a man that admits he makes mistakes.
Someone that will have my back no matter what it takes.
Someone that will walk through fire for me.
Not me always sacrificing for we.
So you see this is what I came up with.
But this is how it is.
I'm in love with my man, but my man love lies elsewhere.
He doesn't on occasions make me smile; he doesn't even look at me he just stares.
As for holding hand, he can't stand to look me in the face.
When loving him was never the case.
He takes what I have and what I have before I get it.
So I asked myself is this the kind of brother I want to end up with, the kind that don't respect me and shit.
I can't pretend I love what you do.
And I can't pretend I'm lost with you.

Inside out

No matter how hard we try to be together, we just can't seem to reunite.
Just to go out alone in it self, is a fight.
I don't understand why he's turning me, every which way but loose.
I don't love him, he doesn't love me, so tell me what's the use.
Just remember your promise, you'll wait no matter what.
There has to be a better way, I can't just sit around and give up.
It has been so long since I've been in the arms of a man that truly cares.
I want to leave all this drama behind, but I'm really scared.
Every night I go to bed, I say this inside my head.

Please remove this evil man from my life and my home.
Make him understand, that he needs to be on his own.
PLEASE remove the hate and fear that I have built inside my heart.
Please remove my devilish ways along with my devilish thoughts.
I'm screaming if you can hear me?
If so answer me please.
If my thoughts are not enough I will release all bad energy.
But just know I'm begging now please find your peace.
Re-invent me into the person that I ought to be.
How did I get here?
What's this all about?
The man I use to love so much has turned me inside out.

It's a wrap

Too many questions and not enough answer yet were still standing here screaming at each other. I'm calling you out your name, you calling me out of my name, we just can't seem to push each other off. You're bitching, I'm always in your face with the same shit everyday not letting you live, when in fact your living two lives. But don't get me wrong, I see myself going to far, pushing your buttons just to get you in my face. Apart of me wishes that you just hit me, at least the feeling will be better than the feeling I'm feeling right now. You don't understand what I'm going through, you can't possibly know all the emotions I'm dealing with. The messed up part is that, I continue to be your lady in the streets, and your freak in the bed. You see I basically rewarded you for screwing up my head.

Now I have to ask myself how much of what you're doing to me is my fault, how much blame am I going to take for this. See accepting you each time you made a mistake showed you, you can treat me anyway you want and I'm still going to be here, because most the time I was. I gave you the ammunition that you used against me. But the only difference now is, you're out of ammunition and I'm fully loaded, you game. You see, I'm given you something you never gave me. I'm given you the option, again that was never given to me. So knowing you're the target are you ready to play this game with me. Are you ready to fight for yours at all cost because I'm prepared to take this at no cost to me at all? Because you see the only loser here tonight is the one that cheated I played by the rules did you, IT'S A WRAP!

Its just comedy, right?

So, this is how it is? This is how you determine you're better than everyone else.
You sit and judge people as they walk by as if you know their worth. Not knowing what that person's been through or even going through.
Not even stopping to think about it or even care.
What is it that makes you judge people you know nothing about?
Is that how you see me behind my back.
Do you judge me and talk about all my faults.
Deciding your perfect and I ain't shit.
Still not knowing a thing about anything.
Really, do you actually think you have the power to decide who's what and who's not?
Do you think your opinion matters, when your life is so screwed up, showing us that you don't feel good unless your making someone else's feel bad.
Do you actually think that shit is funny, and you make friends, believe me when I tell you when people see you they see through you, down to the core of who you really are.
You know what they see when they look at you?
They see a spineless person who's always blowing air.
Some one who lives through others people because there life is so pathetic.
They see someone in crisis but too afraid of being found out, instead of asking for help. That's exactly what they see when they

look at you what do you see when you look at you. Fix yourself up before you start trying to break down someone else, to much work ahead can cause you to get behind.
Then that makes it difficult for you to catch up with yourself.
Stop hating other people's successes because you're too much of a coward to put your best foot forward.
Stop assuming you know what the next person's about. Stop fronting like you got it like that, when in fact your behind in you rent.
Stop pretending you're given us something when really your taking one of the most precious things we have, which is our time, with your tired ass comedy. Girl I would smack you if I didn't feel so bad for you.
Shit, what's the worse part about telling a joke?
When you tell it not realizing it's about you. Damn, that's messed up,
butt it's just comedy right?

Just a little bit.

How serious can it be?
I love outside our union and you loving me.
Giving me a hundred percent of everything you got, and how do I repay you by fucking a man that's everything your not.
He doesn't deserve me and you don't either.
I'm too good for him and not good enough for you, believe me.
I can't seem to stop hurting you; my life is so out of control.
I'm doing 75 in a 25 zone.
Sometimes I believe I deserve to hurt.
I don't put you or our love first.
I thought I was looking at the big picture only to find out I was thinking too small.
I was weighing my options when there shouldn't have been options at all.
I really must be insane.
Hurting a man that gives me everything.
I mean I'm starting to believe what the older folks say.
Women don't want good man nowadays.
They don't appreciate men that step up to the plate
Yet they appreciate the imposters, the pretenders, and the fakes.
I feel like a leach only I'm sucking out the life in you.
And it's not that I don't love you I love you I really do.
It's just right now I can't give you what you need.
I need more time to work on me.
And I love you too much to keep hurting you for no reason at all.

Only thing your guilty of is loving me so hard.
Sometimes we allow our demons to turn us in to something so nasty.
And in return we become our own worse enemy.
You see the funny thing about all this shit.
Because before you came along I was going through it.
I was one of those chicks talking about anit no good men.
When I was questioning good men I should have been questioning my women.
You know what's crazy is I could of ended all this shit.
If I love myself just a little bit.

Just Cause

Do you continue to push even when you're at the edge?
Do you separate yourself, from yourself instead?
How deep does the cut have to be before you're convinced,
that I bleed.
Or is something different this time, should I just follow as you lead.
I should forget the fact that you hit me twice with one punch that wasn't even a jab.
Like you forgot to love the person that loved you real bad.
I have never planned my future and you weren't apart of it.
I be damn if I'm going to keep dealing with this shit.
I do everything except stand on my head.
And you still end up in another woman's bed.
You put my life in the hands of a woman that wasn't even on my level.
My feeling was never considered, you just did whomever.
I'm angry because you put these birds in the mix.
Every time I think about it, I get physically sick.
You allowed a fling to invade my space.
You brought that to my doorstep, what a disgrace.
You call yourself a man, you a damn clown.
Real men uplift their women, not bring them down.
But it's ok, you got that.
But truthfully speaking I don't know if I can ever bounce back.
What do we have, honestly think about it, what we got?
Each other you say, I think not.

I'm so messed up, because for the life of me I can't let go.
I can't walk away, and I don't know why,
yes I do, because you're imbedded in my soul.
You're the first person I loved and the only love I know.
But it doesn't matter you didn't care.
If you did I wouldn't be here.

━━━━━━━━━ Justifiable homicide...

I traveled many roads to get to where I am, and Im still not at home. I keep looking for this certain comfort and I thought I found that comfort with you, only to realize it was your comfort and not mine.

You made me believe you built this life for us, when you built it for you, to control me.

You made me promises that you had no intentions of keeping, only to keep me close.

You abused me mentally and emotionally because you felt I was bigger than our relationship, when in fact I was just loving you harder than you were use to being loved.

I was giving you something so sweet, something honest and pure. You turned that sweet into something sour, you turned my truth into lies.

You turned something that was pure into meaningless gratification, that neither of us is willing to hold onto.

If what I was giving you wasn't enough, why didn't you say so? Why was stripping me, rewarding to you ?

You told me I was your everything, when you loved me like I was nothing.

No matter what you did to me, I stayed, because my love was true, even when you weren't.

You killed everything good in me.

So today I lay to rest that soul, that spirit, that love, that truth, that pure ness that you fought against, all in the name of justifiable homicide.

Killing me slowly

I don't get to see you often, but when I do I cry.
It's because of all the lies you told me that I'm going to die.
Not only is the lie you told me costing me my life.
But the lies you told are also affecting your wife.
When we met I asked if you were married.
You said no, so I was happy about you being in my life, spare me.
If I knew then what I know now, I would of never had you ass around.
You took every chance I had, big and small.
You took my chance of having a family and all.
But that's not the worse part, what about are seed?
The one I have growing inside of me.
Should I bring my baby in this world knowing I'm going to die?
Or should I abort my baby so he/she wouldn't be affected or infected by your lie.

All because you were lying up with guys.
But for whatever reason I can't make up my mind.
I love who I have growing inside.
I loved my baby since the first day I found out.
Now I'll never know what motherhood is about.
This is my life, it belonged to me.
And you took it so cowardly.
Now I'm stuck with a choice to make.
And either way it's a lot at stake.

I love him or her too much to take their life.
It's just no guarantee they'll survive because of my sacrifice.
He or she can still be infected and lose their life?
So is what I'm doing right?
Should I give birth and take that chance?
Or abort my love because of this man.
Why did it ever have to get to this stage?
Why did you infect me with AIDS?

Let me complete me...

Can you see it? It's right there behind my eyes. Can you see it? It's right behind my smile. Can you see it? It's right there in my laugh. Can you see it, because I have.
I noticed it one day, not intentionally but I saw it nonetheless.
Your outside was beautiful, but your inside was a mess.
You were struggling with two people and I only saw one.
Yet it was clear to me that you were battling someone.
No ones sees the hurt in my eyes. The strain in my smile. No one hears the emptiness in my voice. I didn't chose it, I sorta didn't have a choice.
You see I fought like hell to win this fight.
I battled back and forth with wrong and right.
If I forgive you, can I let go.
Can I move onto a love I know.
As much as I hate to admit this, I'm incomplete, not because you think you complete me.
I'm incomplete because you turn me into someone else.
With you I'm just not myself.
I'm stuck some where else when I'm feeling you.
It's not normal going through the crap I'm going through.
Can I breath again, can you set me free.
I don't regret loving you but it's killing me.
I forgive you, now let me breathe.
Let me, give me what I need to complete me.

Let's save our love

I love you too much not to fight to get us back.
Although things may seem final, my heart won't allow me to believe that.
I want us back more than you know.
Our issues is causing us not to grow.
Don't ever think that what I needed was about somebody else.
I had to walk away to save myself.
I needed to know what I had to do, to take care of me.
I needed to get back to my sanity.
I really needed to know if this is where I belonged.
I needed answer as to why things kept going wrong.
I want to know why the man I spent so many years loving, lost sight of me.
What did I do to you to make you feel so incomplete?
I love you with everything in me and I know you feel the same.
Life goes on and sometimes things change.
I refuse to believe the man I fell in love with don't love me no more.
I refuse to believe you'll walk away like we anit worth fighting for.
You said I'm never around or never there.
But that didn't mean I didn't love you or didn't care.
We started our family early and we were so young.
I never really experienced loving someone.
We was forced to grow up fast I was a mom and you were a dad.
But we had each other and things weren't so bad.

As we got older things really started to change, you were different, you weren't the same.
You got comfortable being stuck.
And I felt myself giving up.
I control my ship, I'm the captain.
I'm not going to sit around when I can make shit happen.
Maybe I was gone just a little too much.
But you forgot one thing, I was doing it for us.
I love you more than anything, there is nothing I wouldn't do.
So lets save our love.

Looking for love

Tell me were do I turn when turning around seem so hard.
How do I begin to love when love is like playing cards?
Your dealt a hand your not sure you going to win.
And all you get is a broken heart in the end.
Who'll be there if you can't be there for yourself?
What do you do when you know nothing else?
Why should you be punish for loving so freely.
Is it wrong to give yourself to someone completely?
When you love someone you can't wear a disguise.
They can only believe in what they see in your eyes.
You can't build a relationship build on a lie.
Once you start over watering it, it dies.
You never told me your love came with a price.
You broke my heart, I let you back twice.
I was your trophy that you put on display.
The minute the curtains close, you be on your way.
You treated me so bad, when I was loving you so deep.
But instead of loving me, you chose to creep.
I'm not bitter it was what it was.
Right now, I'm just looking for love.

Love me enough...

You have all these thoughts now that you realized I'm that perfect piece to the puzzle that suddenly fits. I'm your world now that I'm gone. That feeling you feel, its call empty, the same feelings you gave me. You didn't appreciate me until I left, and now you can't live without me. The whole time we were together, I lived without you, and you were right there.

You were suppose to fight for us and all you ever did was contribute to the destruction of us. You lost me way before I left. I can never love you again, the thought of me ever being able to love you, hurts. I can't deal with you, or even with the thought of you hurting me again. Sometimes I don't know what hurts the most, the thought or the actual pain. I developed a mechanism that I use to protect myself, just to remind me you're not worth giving my heart to. Right now I'm feeding my insecurities with all the things that was done to me, so that I can rebuild so that it doesn't happen again because that's all I have. So from this point on, I'm asking that someone love me enough. Love me enough to know I might hurt you, or that I might cheat on you. Love me enough to know that I will put me first. Love me enough to know that what you do or done to me, I might do to you. All I'm asking is that YOU just love me enough.

Love never the same

How do you set aside heartache and sorrow?
When you're too afraid to face tomorrow.
You tell yourself all you need is time away.
Knowing deep down in your heart it's going to be harder to face another day.
I gave my heart to him, thinking it was for eternity.
And my one true love, turned his back on me.
What was I to do, what was I to say.
I can't force him to love me, it's not supposed to be that way.
I feel stuck, trapped and all alone.
It was like magic "POOF" he's gone
Living my life will never be the same.
My heart will hurt at the mention of his name.
How could he love me and cause me so much pain.
I know what I lost, but what did he gain?

Me myself and I

Sometimes I allow other peoples feelings to be more important than mine, even when I know its wrong.
I do it because I don't ever want to be the source of any ones pain.
Their my source of pain, who shields me like I shield them.
I want what I put out, is that wrong.
I would just like for someone else to consider my feeling like I do every body else's.
I mean, I don't do what I do for acknowledgements, but at least be considerate.
Sometimes the strongest person gets weak.
So for now on, I have to show people how I want to be treated.
I have to be considerate of myself if I want others to be as well.
I have to shield myself from people with bad intentions.
I have to be the main source of energy that I want to receive.
My feelings will come first because my feelings are apart of who I am.
So if I'm accepting something other than what I'm putting out.
Than the only one to blame is Me, Myself, and I.

Missing pieces

Your love is good beneath the surface.
But why are we together, what's the purpose.
You know my most precious moment are shadowed by greed.
Begging for love, instead of getting it for free.
You keep telling me how I play a big part in who you are.
Yet for your love, I starve.
I keep insisting you treat me right.
Now I can't help but to feel I'm fighting the wrong fight.
Don't get me wrong, I love you to no end.
Remember before we were lovers, we were friends.
I never once thought I could experience such pain.
By losing a love, I fought so hard to gain.
Why are we here, how did it get this far.
What issues weigh more than the love in our hearts?
I still love you and that will never change.
It's just different now, it's not the same.
It's not the love we once were seeking.
It's love now with missing pieces.

Miss us with the bullshit...

How is it that every police officer got off for killing a unarmed black man.
Is that the plan, kill them all while you can.
Take there life, it don't matter anyway.
That's their thought, but that's not what they'll say.
No justice for the unjust, just a few drops of shit on their name, just because they have a record they you feel they have the right to be slain.
We pay taxes for you to protect and serve and make us feel safe and secure.
Yet who's protecting our fathers brothers and sons from legal gangstas that's killing them more.
Cameras are not enough, when the truth is right there.
It's never justifiable they just don't care.
Now people are fighting back and the world is on edge.
I can only imagine what's going through there head.
The law wasn't designed for the black man, it was designed to keep the black man imprisoned, even when their free.
The law was designed for the privilege, not the ones that share the same color as me.
Don't be surprise when we star fighting back.
Protecting ourselves against your their attacks.
Some people really don't get it.
When just want justice, miss us with the bullshit.

My gentle giant

I have a gentle giant larger than life to me.
Big and strong and humble, gentle as man can be.
His voice is strong, but light as whisper, barely loud enough to hear.
Yet I have a strong sense of security whenever my giant is near.
I mean don't get me wrong, he's a man he's not perfect, but he's a king in my eyes.
No matter what we go through I know what he feels inside.
He has his moments, like we all do.
My gentle giant loves me, and I love my gentle giant to.
We created something together, that no one will ever tear apart.
They might get inside our heads but they'll never get inside our hearts.
I'm making new vows to him right now.
I vow to love him to the day they put me in the ground.
I promise to share everything with him good or bad.
I promise to leave the past mistakes in the past.
And I loved him for twenty-one years and I want twenty-one more.
Because the kind of love we got it's worth fighting for.
So as you see I love my gentle giant he means the world to me.
And without my gentle giant I just don't feel complete.
I have a gentle giant that's larger than life too me.
Big and strong and humble, gentle as a man can be.
His voice strong, but light as whisper, barely loud enough to hear.
Yet I have a sense of security whenever my giant is near.

I mean don't get me wrong, he's a man he's not perfect, but he's king in my eyes.
No matter what we go through, I know what he feels inside.
He has his moments like we all do.
My gentle giant loves me, and I love my gentle giant to.

My little secret

Day to day activity becoming lighter and easier to bare.
Not that it's better, but I can't see it if I'm not there.
Not choosing to ignore it, but just not think about it now.
It still matters, but I don't feel it when I'm not around.
So if a little distance is all it takes.
I'll do that if it means were still in the race.
I'm not trying run this race alone.
But don't think for once I can't make it on my own.
I posses something a few woman have.
I owned it since I was fourteen and boy is it bad.
I don't have to explain it you'll know what it is as soon as I open my mouth.
Trust me you'll know what I'm talking about.
But for now it will remain a secret of mine.
It will come to surface in due time.
Don't rush it that won't be a good ideal.
A secret expose to fast is a secret to real.
I mean a secret leaked, is a cover blown.
And if you're not prepared, leave it alone.
You heard the saying don't dip your feet in the water if you don't want to get them wet.
Don't expose a secret that's not ready yet.

My pledge allegiance

I built so many walls around myself so that nothing or no one can hurt me.
I was so busy trying to keep the unwanted pain out, that I forgot to build and exit to escape when the pain finally reaches me.
Now that it's here, I have nowhere to go except backwards.
Now I have to knock down these walls and rebuild over so that I can survive.
I have to separate my pain from my anger, which is sometimes hard to do when their one in the same.
Most of the time I feel like it's me against the world and the world is winning because I don't know what the fight is about.
I find myself losing control and there's nothing I can do about it because I'm stuck.
I mentally created a jail that I can't seem to get out of.
My only crime is, I chose to love someone who apparently didn't love me.
I trusted someone who didn't trust himself.
I believed if you loved someone you compromise.
Is that a joke or what?
I compromised my whole life, and were has it gotten me.
Sometimes I'm afraid to open my eyes because apart of me wants to believe it's a dream, but it not, it's real and I'm afraid to address it.
I'm afraid that I might say the wrong thing and he'll get up leave.
It's not even about him leaving, as much as it is about me being by myself.

What am I suppose to do just forget about the last few years.
Pick up were I left off before the infection seeped in.
How do I let years go when I think to myself that I shoulda fought harder to hold on?
Maybe I was safer when the walls was up and nowhere to go.
Maybe I was enabling him instead of helping him.
You know what the problem is I keep making excuses for him treating me like the shit he scraped off the bottom of shoes.
Why should I be looking for ways to fix it when I didn't mess it up?
Why should I have to protect myself from a man that suppose to love me?
Why should I have to create a place within myself to be normal or abnormal, which ever comes first, because everyday is different?
Why should I react to his mistakes?
Why should I pull myself out of character when I'm in a place were honesty is not issue.
So what is it that has me spinning in circles trying to catch my tail?
Is it the reason for all our misunderstandings and your tantrums that's been going on lately.
Or is it just the case of you draining the well dry.
How could I have been so unfair?
Why am I always looking for worst in you when I think our lives are being tampered with?
Why should you catch the jist of it all when in fact I 'm shaking the walls I built around me?
I guess you never really get over being taken for a fool.
When you love your man and you find out you're servicing your man.
And he laid up somewhere else.
You can accept the fact that it happens but you'll always remember it did.
And it doesn't make me love you any lesser.
It just makes you more aware of what's going on around you.

My reflection of you

Mama I tried so many times to get close to you.
You wouldn't allow me to lean on you; the love just wouldn't come through.
Ma chasing a man was like a job to you, only you didn't get paid and the bills mounted up too.
You left me to fend for myself.
You didn't care about me only yourself.
You allowed the streets to embrace me as if I was it's own.
Prostituting was my way of life and the streets became my home.
You didn't care that at the age of fourteen I was forced down on my knees.
He said suck my dick bitch until your knees bleed.
You know what he did after that, he pissed on me, left me laying there as if I was nothing.
Did I mention this happen the first night I was forced on the streets.
Because my second night was worse I had a gang of them on me.
On the third night I became wise.
I was aware of what I had between my thighs.
The first few nights it made me sick.
But I started taking care of myself by turning tricks.
Many of nights I couldn't look myself in the face, because I was scared of what I might see.
Then I remembered I was the prostitute but the prostitute wasn't me.
For every three hundred I made I put two away.

I pulled myself up by the bootstraps I was determined not to be that way.
I didn't need you or my dad all I needed was time.
And you know what, I got mine.
I put myself back in school and got my g.e.d
Put myself through college and got my associate degree.
Did I mention I'm a wife and a mother of three?
I got it together mom because your weakness will not defy me.
You know what's sad at the age of fourteen I had to do what I had to do.
But what's even sadder is when the one person you depend on, walks out on you.
Mom I want to thank you.
You only did what you came so accustom to.
I'm just glad that now when I look in the mirror I see me my reflection is no longer of you.

New Orleans unseen

God bless America the home of the red white and blue.
Um um um the last I checked New Orleans is apart of America, yet they got know love they were left to fend for themselves.
Don't get me wrong we get down for us but what can you do with no resources.
Those Kat's drops the ball and now they want to act like they don't know were to lay the blame.
Everybody pointing fingers forgetting they're four pointing back?
When our they going to realize we see them for the way they see us.
We dropped the blinders along time ago.
Lives were lost because they thought light over dark.
I can't phantom the ideal that you Kat's can sleep at night.
This country was built on the back of a black man.
Yet you keep asking us to close our eyes and turn our heads while you run the shit in the ground.
What happen to liberty and justice for all?
What does the word FREE mean to you?
Out of sight out of mind.
So many lives lost and hearts broken and spirits gone. The pain in their eyes would never be forgotten.
Everyone lost something during that tragedy.
You can't be human and not feel that pain.
And pretending that the urgency signs weren't there isn't going to bring back the hundreds of people that lost their lives.

It's not going to replace the fact that a mother and father have lost their child, or the fact that a child has lost their parents.
It doesn't erase the fact that New Orleans was left for dead.
WHAT'S GOING ON why can't you see us?

Paused

All my life I just
Paused.

Pick up games

I stand here today defeated and tired of fighting someone else's demons.
Tired or trying to right someone else's wrong. When I stand and face the mirror I see a woman of light complexion with sunken in eyes deflated jaws and light whispers. I see a woman that forgot to love herself while trying to love someone that strips her of everything. My reflection should be a woman of light complexion inflated jaws and perky eyes and butterfly whispers, that's the reflection I should see. I would have never thought you would commit such hard fouls against me. I guess you can since I never call you on any thing. I don't call you on your double dribbling, your walking or charging. But I bear the mark for each foul you committed against me. My heart is still bleeding from the flagrant foul that was really unnecessary. Believe it or not I was posted inside and you were behind me with plenty room to shoot, but you refuse yet it didn't stop you from running up the middle. Did you forget basketball is a team sport, you belong to a team but you keep picking up these one on ones.
Damn we've played three quarters and I still don't know the name of your team. My teams committed yours, undecided. My job as your teammate is not to leave you open. Unlike you I stick to guarding my man, you keep sticking and moving that's boxing you have to know your position either you sticking or moving. Evidently your sticking because I'm constantly being left open.

After running three quarters and half of 4th I'm tired and really exhausted.
I'm sending in a sub I've had enough it's about time I watch from the sidelines. I guess the saying is true if you can't be with the one you love, love the one you with. Because every one on one you have I find it easier and easier to ride the bench.

Prisoner 24-7-365

24-7-365 was my state number and boy was I catching hell.
You would of thought I was a prisoner in a county jail.
I was charged with giving my heart.
Letting a weak ass man rip me apart.
Making sure he left me with little or no hope.
Had me feeling as if I was at the end of my rope.
His words were like crack to the average geezer.
Had me believing I really needed him.
He had me convinced that I wouldn't amount to shit.
And the worse part was I believed it.
I got paroled in 89.
And released permanent in 95.
He mistook my kindness for weakness.
With him I felt the bitter sweetness.
His love left a bitter taste in my mouth.
He didn't love me he was turning me the fuck out.
I gave him control and he did what he did.
He didn't treat me like his woman he treated me like his kid.
He abused everything sacred I gave to him.
He even abused what I had hidden inside.
I gave him control over my life and that's how I became prisoner 24-7-365

Raped

I was raped not physically but mentally to many times.
That nigger took from me what the both of us should have treasured.
Surrounding me with material things that suppose to make me feel good until you were able to come around.
Promising me that we were going to be together knowing you had no intentions on making me a permanent fixture in your life.
You were allowed to come to me as you pleased.
You had me believing you loved me, when in fact you were raping me.
I believed you loved me so it didn't matter when you came as long as you were there.
I was experiencing something different with you.
I really thought it was love.
I convinced myself that it was love but I was just being naïve and you were being a predator.
Some people have the nerve to question me about my mental state because I can't seem to separate my past from my future.
I'm blaming everyone except you.
I'm destroying everything I love because I can't confront you.
I can't come to grips with the fact I couldn't separate the two
LOVE/RAPE
Damn, you mentally raped me

Say it's worth saving

Sometimes what you fight so hard to hold onto is the one thing you should let go of.
You don't let go because your heart tells you it's worth holding onto. Then you fight with everything in you only to find that you are fighting by yourself and to fight alone is fighting against yourself. And when you fight against yourself you lose.
Yet you hold on anyway. I've been through fire with you and I didn't turn into ash then and I'm not now, forever means forever. I truly don't know if I can exist without you. Like things, people suffer a lot of wear and tear to.
It's just not visible to every one. I can't let go because if I let go I'll feel like I'm letting go apart me. If you say we can't fix this, I'll walk away and never look back. If you tell me we can fix this and I'll stay and fight the fight. Tell me the tears I cried so many nights was worth what we had. Tell me I'm not crazy for loving you the way I do.
I grew up loving you, your love is all I know. I 'm not going to pretend things hasn't happen, but I can't pretend that I don't love you either. We both did things that we weren't proud of, but you never stop loving me and I never stop loving you. I feel in love with you because you knew how to love me, you gave me what I needed when I needed it and you loved me more than you hurt me. I didn't fall in love because you was perfect
You're not perfect, no one is. As long as you keep loving me and doing right by me I will continue to love you and have your back.

And If tell you I'm going to be there believe me, and I tell you it's over, believe that to. You know what kind of woman you have I don't have to tell you that right. That night your boy said that I must bring out the worst in you that fucked me up because here I was thinking we brought the best out in each other. Then I start to remember the times we brought the worst out in each other. I use to purposely try to push your buttons to get you fired up but you never would.

I remember wanting to get you angry just so I can say I hate you. But for the life of me I couldn't hate you half as much as I loved you. As bad as I wanted to leave I couldn't, my chest would hurt whenever I think I got the heart up to ask you to leave. Then it hits me I love you to much to hate you.

We are the reason things are the way they are. We allowed other people in now its are job to keep them out. If you say we can't fix this then I'll turn and walk away. If you say we can fix this then I stay and fight the fight. Just say it's worth saving.

Secret garden

You can't plant something and then not water it, and expect it to grow. Anything you plant you must nurture it. Just like you can't watch something grow and not appreciate the changes it goes through. We can't get mad because something we nurtured is shedding layers and we don't like it. We have to learn to appreciate growth even when it stops growing. Just because we planted the seeds, watered and nurtured it and watched it grow, doesn't mean we have the right to keep it to ourselves.

Once we spoke existence into the bulb so it can shine, its only right that we let it blossom.

Be proud of what you planted and nurtured.

And what ever you don't agree with add to your secret garden.

Securing our daughters childhood

Why would a mother turn her back on her daughter so innocence and so young.
Without the proper guidance she'll be sprung before she's twenty-one.
And we know at the tender age of fourteen life begins for her.
So we as mothers can't allow our daughters to suffer.
We have to remember when we use to laugh and joke and crying was ok to.
Remember how you build it so you know what to do to keep it from coming unglued.
I want my daughters to know they can come to me for anything.
To just talk laugh or even comforting.
I don't want the spot she hold her books to be replaced by the spot she'll hold a baby.
See it's our job to see that they grow into respectable young ladies.
I guess what I'm trying to say they have their hold life ahead of them.
We can't allow temptation to pull them in.
We have to work hard at letting them know they only get one childhood.
We just can't allow them to walk blindly in adulthood.
I want my daughters to be able to do things kids their age do.

I want them to have fun growing up but at the same time remain true.
I also want them to be aware of how body and heart works.
I don't want them to fall in love to soon and end up getting hurt.
I want them to know a guy will tell whatever it is you want to hear.
It gives them a better chance at keeping our babies near.
You know what' going to happen, she'll be pregnant in less than year.
Inform them now let them know the repercussions in producing.
Please don't allow them to damage their future.
Mom's please don't allow are babies to make the same choices we made.
Let them know there will be know debts that go unpaid.
But most of all remind them that we our there for them.
For good and bad and from the beginning to the end.

Sex, lies and secrets

What happens in the dark, always to come to light?
To you it was just sex, to her it was more than a night.
Because of that night, things will never be the same.
Her heart will break, whenever she hears your name.
You used her for sex by telling her lies.
How is that cool and it can't be justified.
Something as small as a firecracker, can blow up like a dynamite if smother long enough.
It can cause casualties when you messing it up.
Secrets have a way of sneaking out of your subconscious and landing on the surface exposing you to the world.

Truth be told, lies unfolds and secrets consumes you and sex just wear you the fuck out.
Then again its just sex lies and secrets right.

So far away...

As I lay here looking up at the ceiling, I realize how much you are deeply missed. Your touch, your voice and your warm kiss. I miss the way you play the game. I miss the way you whisper my name. I thought I was ok with you being away. Only to realize that I miss you more than words can say. I miss the way you smile at me. I miss the way we use to be. I remember the time we laughed so much you said you couldn't breathe. Yet you caught just enough air to confess your love to me. Remember the night I cried so hard for no reason at all. And you held me and told me you will always be here to break my fall. I'm falling baby, catch me before I hit the ground. Keep your word my love, don't let me down. Don't let mistakes keep us apart. Come feel this empty space I have in my heart. Put your body back in this spot next to me. This is were you suppose to be. I don't know my night from my days, because the man I love so much, is so far away.

So High

As I walk the streets of my neighborhood at 9'oclock at night, I should be kind of scared, but for some reason I'm not.
Tonight my mood is different, fear is the last thing on my mind. The last few years has been rough, but we stayed on course and fought right through it.
It also made me realize that you can't take anything for granted, especially friendship, is so important in a relationship. Without it you lose sight on what got you there in the first place.

You are going to go through so many ups and downs in your relationship, but only you and that person that you are in the relationship with can determine how it ends.
You can't say you love someone and then ask someone who has nothing to do with it, what they think.
You can't give other people a say in how you handle your relationship.
A couple is two, don't bring in someone that has no right to be there.

After all the lies, and broken promises, we found each other again.
We learned how to be friends again and it saved our relationship. We were able to be honest with each other, we were able to say everything and not suffer from a backlash, because friendship is the safe place in our relationship.
It was like I was seeing him for the first time, seeing myself.

I saw something some where and it said somethings to this affect, if the same person you love is the same person that hurts you than you have something.
I wouldn't say I agree with that, but I do know the person you love will be the person that hurts you the most.
You just have to ask yourself, do I love us more than I hate us.
I did, I loved us more than the tears he put my eyes and the pain he put in my heart.

When you truly love someone there is nothing you wouldn't do to save your relationship.
No matter how much it hurts, when you love someone you do whatever it takes.
You go that extra mile for the ones we love.
And because I love him more than I can say.
I'm glad I fought the fight.
I reintroduced myself to and old friend, now we get to experience this love on another level…So High

Someday we'll be free...

I sit and watch how we all get caught up in this twisted plot to destroy us. Only to fall into it by destroying each other.

Pettiness is a sign of weakness, would you show a thief where you're jewels are, so why show the world your weakness.

We're vulnerable to other races because we're to afraid to help our own succeed.

We have so much hate and jealous amongst our own, that we don't realize if one of us is up, we all winning.

I never seen anyone one stand up to something sitting down with there hands tide behind their back.

We would rather give our money to people that don't respect us, then spend it in a black own business because you hate seeing your sister and brothers up.

We have made every slave owner rich by being a pawn in a game we ain't suppose to play.

We're constantly being traded and sold, yet we keep paying them to do it.

Wake up people, we keep sleeping on the wrong things and grasping shit that's meant to break us.

Open your eyes, we're slaves to a fashion that wasn't made for us, but built off the sweat of are backs.

Damn I might not be here it to witness it, but someday we'll be free.

Speechless

I am a woman you better recognize.
Don't be fool by the look in my eyes.
What I say will hit you and cause you to daze.
I'm realer than your homie, and sharper then a switchblade.
Now I might look soft as flower.
But believe, I pack a lot of power.
I'm not talking power in street.
I'm talking power in speech.
You see mentally you're not ready to mess with a woman of my caliber, I'm as real as they come.
You came for me, but I'm not the one.
You thought I was easy and wasted no time,
Coming for me about one of mine.
Fifty was talking about you when he made wanksta.
You soft as a cream puff trying to play gangsta.
Man I really didn't think I was going to have to pull your card.
Here go mister softy trying to play hard.
Fronting like a man when you really a bitch.
Gossiping like a woman telling secrets and shit.
Telling me one thing, and doing another.
What should have been personal was shared with others.
You a mark, coming at you is way to easy.
Even though you provoked me talking greasy.
Yo hold up I'm giving you way to many lines.
Ten is thinking about you so let's stop at nine
Let this be the last time I address this mess.
This time you were safe, only left speechless.

Starting fresh

You came to me at the wrong time, you came to me at my crucial point.
You came at a time I couldn't decide what I want.
It had been a year since I loss the love of my life.
And reminders was like losing him twice.
He was my everything, and I was his.
We made plans together to have kids.
We tied the knot in Aug. 2006
The most beautiful day, I will never forget.

A year into our marriage, he was on his way to work, a truck sideswiped his car sending it flipping off the road.
At that very moment I was standing in the kitchen and something shifted in my soul.
The phone rung, I picked it up and the voice on the other end said, its been an accident and he's at the hospital, get here real quick.
I jumped in my car and held my head and instantly became sick.
Man can you imagine all the things running through my mind.
Thinking out loud, this can't be his time.
I get to the hospital room where my heart laid, I stood frozen, stuck in a daze.

As I was standing there, the machine started to beep.
My one true love, was slipping away from me.

The doctor said he was sorry he did all that he can.
I was standing there looking him in his eyes, not hearing a word he was saying.
So you see, I can't promise you my heart.
If it ok with you, can we get a fresh start.

Suicidal thoughts

Confused, withdrawn and my need to smoke, shows just how out of it I really am. I'm no longer making choices that concern others, except the lives I'm responsible for. I'm no longer looking for the approvals of others; it's my life, I'll live the way I see fit. I'll have the final say regarding me and my heart and my soul.
My fate will not be determined by man's flesh.
I'll have the final say in whom I choose to sleep with directly, or indirectly.
Your worth will not determine mine; justice is not for you but for me.
I'll drive the ship from now on, and you walk the plank.
I shouldn't have to swim in waters you ran.
I am not going to allowed how you carry yourself in the streets determine who I am.
You will not sacrifice a piece of me for a piece of you.
I'm in a place were I can catch myself before falling.
I don't have to share that walk with you.
I didn't draw blood, you did, because what was once connected to me was torn from me as well.
I refuse to go under with you, myself respect is my life jacket, and I love myself more than I love you.
But because I was blinded by love, I gave you the power you had over me, now I'm taking it back I'll decide for me while you keep deciding for yourself.
Your love has caused me to have suicidal thoughts; so watching you walk it alone shows me I survived being suicidal and not even knowing it.

Trapped inside

Sometimes I feel like a bird with clipped wings. Walking and running when I know I should be soaring.
Feeling caged, when I know I'm free.
Expecting the unexpected but getting nothing. Dreaming in color, but living in black and white.
Choosing my battles, only to lose the fight.
They say, time waits for no one, that I believe.
It changes like seasons, turns like leaves.
How can you claim a lifetime, in two years?
We're suffering cause pain, and the unknown cause feared.
Sometimes our darkness leads us into a place that's tight, and you have no room to move. Escaping only to be confused.
If your tapped out, where does it all come from, and how much change.
Bits and pieces, while acknowledging your shame.
How do you lock down a empty space?
How does a heart vanish and not leave a trace?
Some days I wish I could hide.
This comes from being trapped inside.

Truth be told.

If I have to walk away and never look back, I would be ok with that. I haven't lost a minute of sleep. You created this with the sharp edges of your tongue. You placed me on a cutting board and cut me from every angle, knowing I was tender. You thought verbally beating me down would make me understand how you feel. Nope, it just harden my heart. When you drew blood, you should of stopped, but no, the lashing continued and the cuts got deeper. I will tell you this, I will never look at you the same way, I will never care for you the way I cared before. I can't imagine you ever being lucky in life or love, because you have malicious intent. You think after a few weeks you can say sorry and everything would be ok. You thought because you were forgiving in the past and or I say that's just who he is and let go. Well that's not who I am. I will not allow, you bad to affect the good part of me. I will not allowed you to make me feel guilty because you are miserable. I did not bring misery to you, you did that on your own. Misery will always be a factor as long as you stay cold. Truth be told. You need to learn to love you.

The biggest C in relationship

(Commitments)

I'm concern, yet confused, but I can't seem to put my hands on what it is I'm bothered by the most. Is it the way I say committed and you can't seem to commit to anything? You turned what I thought should have been ours into something so countless and disgusting. You chose greed over love and that meant to me that you couldn't love me enough to be faithful. I was never enough for you huh. You always need or should I say, wanted more. I know for a fact that I filled you up, so it was just a case of you being greedy. Why couldn't you be what I needed when I needed you? Why was hurting me okay? Why didn't you feel something when you had her legs up in the air? While, I was at home washing your clothes and cooking your food. Why was satisfying your dick more important than me. I gave you more than enough of everything. I was your shoulder when you needed someone to lean on. I was that wall that often held you up. I gave you strength when you were at your weakest. So this betrayal wasn't about me, but you. You don't love yourself enough to believe someone can love you unconditional.

I believe you love me, but I also believe your scared. Your not use to someone loving you, I loved you and you hurt me. That's what usually happens to you right. You're screwed up, you take when you should be given. Why did I expect you to love me, when you're not capable of loving yourself?

I'm no longer concerned, confused, or even feeling accountable. I didn't feel the need to rescue you, only myself. I refuse to feel sorry for you. I'm no longer going to apologize for you being hurt by someone else. I'm not going to tell you I understand, when it's really not for me to understand anyway.

I'm not going to lose me, while helping you, find you. I'm more important.

I'm not settling anymore. I'm not concern or confused and most of all I'm not sad, I'm safe.... For the first time in a long time I'm safe...

The mire image

Do you rock when you've been pushed?
Do you fall when you've been tripped?
Do you bleed when you've been cut?
Do you see when your eyes are shut?
Do you go when you can't move?
Do you hold if you don't have arms?
Do you stand if you don't have legs?
You know the answer to all those questions, and you can't see what's right in front of your face.
Sometimes what you see is the mire image of what it suppose to be like.
You have the answer for everything, except the answers you need for yourself.
You sound like a lost child in grocery store who can't find their mother.
Panicking and screaming, not knowing what to do next, spinning in circles just to see if you can get a glimpse or hear their mother yelling out.
What you don't know is you have been rescued, your mother's here now, you can relax, but your still spinning in circles.
Stop pretending to be that child in the grocery store.
Stand firm and you can't be rocked.
Hold steady and you won't fall.
Stop hurting your heart won't bleed.
Stop shutting your eyes and you will see.

If you're moving you will go.
Your arms are your heart that's the part that holds.
And your pride is your legs stand on that alone.
Those are the answer to the questions that's right in front of you.
It's the mire imagine of what it suppose to be.

The naked truth...

The last time I checked, love didn't have a expiration date on it. It didn't even have a lock or unlock code, it was given so freely that it ended up costing people more than they wanted to invest. It gave people some people hope, while others wallowed in all the things that went wrong, that they didn't see when it was right in front of them. They focused on all the i did, and missed out on all the I do's. Some people are so afraid to expose themselves that they don't realize they're hiding the best part of them. How can you speak the words I can't find love, when so many times it was right in your face and you walked past it. Your so blinded by what's on the surface, that you don't see what's in plain sight. How can you put love in the same category as fucking when, the difference is in strokes. As a child you learn the difference in good and bad touch. So when you force your way to the front line a layered up, people don't see the real you. When you stand in the back of the line, layers free showing flaws and all, people see you. Instead of hiding, you exposed who you are, and at the same time you told the world, this is who I am. Stop being afraid to shed each layer that don't represents you. When you expose you, no one else can. So remember being naked tells a lot about you and being fully cloth tells me you're hiding something.

The same addicts with different addictions

You said I'm addict because I like to blow tree's.
Knowing you're addictions keeps you down on your knee's.
Don't try to classify me, when you can't classify yourself.
When you think loving yourself is screwing every one else.

And you how dare you say I love to choke more than I love to breathe.
You have been here my whole life, and still don't know me.
When in fact, your addiction is worse than mine.
On payday you strip your man of his manhood and pride.

And you miss holier than thy, you committed a few sins.
You done something, that struck me as odd, you crucified me as if I was god.

But for the addict I need to confront the most.
The one who shoots liquid in her vain, you know dope.
The one that steals everything that's not nail down.
The one that thinks her reflection is what she sees on the ground.

To call me and addict and not think I'll say a word.
Is like ridding the world of all the birds.

Not saying my addiction is all right.
My addictions don't keep me up all night.
My addictions don't have me looking bad.
My addictions don't have me selling my ass.
My addiction doesn't take food out of my kids my mouth.
And my addiction doesn't have me pretending, I'm not turned out.

You see what you started playing games.
And it all started when you said we were the same.
To call me an addict was like spitting in face.
I didn't call you on anything I stayed in my place.

Oh girlfriend, don't think I forget about you.
You're addiction is pitiful to.
You're addicted to telling lies.
Thinking you really getting by.
I don't ever remember a time, you were real.
Many of nights we heard you squeal.

Yeah you didn't think I was going to go off like this.
Truthfully speaking, you got me pissed.
To throw stones at me, and you live in a glass house.
What did you think we would be talking about.

So maybe we are the same addicts with different addictions.

The scenario

Digging for away out, but I can't get past the mud that lies in front of my door.
No matter how hard I try, it's always something sitting in my way.
So infested with the everyday shit, that I find myself wanting to dip.
Sometimes I get so messed up mentally, I can't get past my own truth.
I pretend to be listening, when in reality I'm zoned out.
To me your truth doesn't matter because at than end the night were still going to be unfaithful, untruthful.
Do what works for you.
What works for you, it just might work for me as well?
I'm willing to leave the door cracked, but it's up to you who get's in.
I can't sit here and tell you I'll wait for you, because I wouldn't ask you to wait for me, the thought alone is just selfish.
I keep giving you the remix version of what's going down when in fact I should give it to you raw.
But something tells me you can't handle the truth, my truth anyway.
You see what you did to me is no different than what I'm doing to you.
Only difference is, I'm not pissing on you and telling you it's raining.
You know everything I do, after I do it, it's the American way.

So you feel me when I tell you what works for you might work for me as well.
In a way we're out searching for the same things, love has got one of us messed up., anytime you give a label to your side jawn.
You see I don't think you want to call this what it really is do you.
So let's just say you beat me, but I defeated you and with who's truth.
But if you think about it, this is just a scenario.

This is love

Come on give me what you got.
To you it isn't much, to me it's a lot.
I crave for you like a pregnant women craves for food.
Only I don't eat you, just breathe in the scent of you.
Your love is so intoxicating that sometimes I'm dizzy for hours.
And if you're not around it's like I'm stripped of my super powers.
I've never loved anyone as much as I love you.
I mean you're the only one I was ever willing to commit my life to.
Sometimes I truly feel like were twins.
Because when you hurt, I feel the pain you're in.
I know what you're going to say before it comes out your mouth.
I know what you mean, when others don't know what you're talking about.
Sometimes I don't know where I start or you end.
But I know life together is full of new beginnings.
I really feel in my heart that we'll stand the test of time.
Because your love is all I feel inside.
Sometimes I can't wait to go to sleep, just to wake up again.
Just so I can look at you and take you all in.
I can't catch my breath once I whisper your name.
All I know is, since loving you, things hasn't been the same.
The love I have for you, is the real thing.
My love, you're my everything.
You are like the blood in my veins.
The letters in my name.

The shit that makes a person go insane.
You traveled roads, so long and so cold.
To reach a destination, down in my soul.
I can't remember what my life was like, before you came along.
All I know if you're not in it, it's all wrong.
This is love.

True luv

You can see a lot, when looking through the eyes of others.
Sometimes it's amazing what you discover.
To bad you give them what you don't see.
Judging them out of curiosity.
Figuring, before you start adding.
Subtracting, never really equaling.
At least that's the message you send.
When loving with a closed mouth, keeping it all in.
Since you don't know let me explain.
The fact that you don't know is just insane.
Have you ever heard of dedication to self.
Do you know the difference in, love and sex?
Do you really no what it feels like to make love to your self?
When I get into something, I go all the way.
I don't walk away, I'm here any time of the day.
The one true love in your life, should be you.
Be careful with what you allow yourself to go through.
I'm not trying to get you confused.
But your one true luv should always be you.

Twenty eight days

My footsteps match the sound of my heart beat.
Yet it don't sound strong, almost weak.
My legs start trembling and got a little numb.
I reached out for balance and I had none.
My head started feeling a little light.
I'm functioning like I'm losing the fight.
I can hear my heart beating inside my ear.
It's like I'm feeling my last breath near.
So I guess this is what it feel likes not to exist.
To just be the shell of someone that no one miss.
Realistically this is how I felt when I confronted you with issues about us.
You played with my emotions and you abused my trust.
You kept making me feel smaller and smaller each time you lied.
Yet I can't get over how you kept lying, looking me in the eyes.
I felt like I was in another world stuck in a haze.
And all I can remember was you saying, I was tripping due to the cycle I get every twenty-eight days.
You blamed everyone but you.
It was my fault I was going through the shit I was going through.
You dismissed my pain, a tried to cover it with lies.
You didn't care that only a shell was there and I wasn't inside.
Yet all I can remember was you saying I was tripping due to the cycle I get every twenty-eight days.

I guess it was the cycle I get every twenty-eight days that caused me to let some one else inside my heart.

I believe it was the cycle that I get every twenty-eight days that caused me to move on and get a new start.

I guess it was my cycle that caused some one else to wipe my tears away.

The same cycle that caused you to stray.

I'm much happier now; he treats me like a queen.

He loves me for me and honesty is everything.

So I guess it was the cycle I get every twenty-eight days that caused him to love me.

The same cycle that causes me to love him unconditionally.

We got that love Jones

I get so caught up in you when we having conversations, that I sometimes don't hear a word you say.
And when we're apart, I find myself wishing you was here because I'm missing you like crazy.
My days are incomplete if I don't hear from you at least 4 times, until I'm next to you.
I often find myself thinking about you when clearly I'm suppose to be doing something else.
Thoughts of you consume so much of me, I don't know whether I'm coming or going.
I do know when we apart you are all I think about.
Sometimes I find myself writing your name out in my food.
I'm so hooked on you, I think I would need rehab to let you go.
You have given me this feeling I have never experienced before.
I wash my sheets in your oils, so when your not here I still have the scent of you right here with me.
I have your picture on my phone so that you will never be far away.
Even when you here I feel like we are not close enough.
I sound like a infatuated stalker in love with a man that's not mine lol, that's not the case.
I'm just a wife that has a real bad love jones for her husband.

What is love?

Is there really only one answer for that question?
Love is what you give from the inside.
Love is a numerous of things.
Love is a circle, in form of a ring.
Love can be pretty and ugly, yet love can be, oh so lovely.
Love is letting go, even when it hurts.
Love is work.
Love is a ugly truth, wrapped in a deceitful package, with a gorgeous ribbon.
Love is forgiving.
Love is free, but we often pay.
Love is honesty, some might say.
Love is mental, spiritual and emotional.
Love is uncontrollable.
Love isn't physical, anybody can fuck.
Love is never giving up.
Love is being able to love past mistakes.
Love is what you give, not what you take.
These are the thoughts that runs through my head.
What is love?
Is chivalry dead?

What's your position?

Why can't you be truthful with the words you speak?
Why should I have to sit and figure out if its some truth to what you say.
Your position is to back me in whatever I do, whether you like it or not.
You banging your fist against your chest calling yourself a man fumbling each time the ball is put in your hands.
I'm not going to talk about the tantrums you through cause let you tell it you're never dealt a good hand.
Why can't you accept the fact that no matter what kind of hand your dealt you fold anyway?
Why can't you be truthful with the words you're speaking?
What is it that you're really seeking?
You trying to tell me shit between us are fine.
When so many times you crossed the line.
You so quick to swing and even quicker to strike out.
Yet you still think you have the right to keep running your mouth.
You said you were the hats, and the pants.
Then you better step up and be the man.
I've been blocking for you for as long as I could.
We have been going back and forth about nothing, this shit is no good.
So maybe it's me that's out of line.
So excuse me but what position are you playing this time.

When it hurt so bad, and feels so good.

As I walk away from what seems like my whole life, I can't help but smile at all the memories. I was thinking back to the time you said let me get a little taste, and that taste turned into a 4 hour love session. I also remember the time I was sitting on the back porch, and you came up and began kissing me so passionately, causing me to stand and stumble backward toward the wall. As I leaned in for a more deeper kiss, your hands started to roam up and down my body causing me to flutter. I tried to push off, but the kiss became more passionate. As I gripped you tighter I m becoming winded, but aggressive at the same time. I began biting at your neck and ripping open your shirt, placing soft kisses on your chest while roughly grinding into your manhood. You flipped the script back to you, because I was taken control, and it was your show. I remember exactly how you did it. You pushed me back in to the wall while gripping my neck with one hand, and snatching my panties off with the other in one smooth motion. As you inserted your fingers inside my box I moaned with pleasure, it sent a surge that made me quiver. I remembered how I began riding your fingers as I moved my body in circular motion. I'm smiling thinking about those soft kisses you were gently laying on my lips as your fist pounded my mound. As I open my eyes and part my lips I drop to my knees to catch the son or daughter that neither of us could afford. As your sweetness runs down my lips and chin, I ran my tongue across what remains. As I stand, I can't help but look into your eyes and see the love before you spoke the words, and landed that forehead kiss. Wow the memories alone brings life back into this love affair that slowly faded. It's hard when it hurts so bad, but feels so good.

When the cut is so deep, it never stops bleeding...

You ever heard someone say, physically I'm here, mentally, I left a long time ago. That's real talk right there. I seen it happen so many times. Not because you stop loving someone, but because you were forced to see just how much that someone loved you. You give a person the most intimate part of you, and they turn around and hurt you, for someone that meant nothing. All the baby I'm sorries, don't make up for the pain you feel. The easiest part is that you forgive, and the hardest part is you never forget. It wouldn't be so bad if they didn't paint that beautiful picture of forever, and tell you, your the only one for them. Who you did, will never hurt as much as what you did? When I think about where we stand and where we stood, all I can do is cry. Where were you when I needed you here with me? Why was getting your dick wet more important than me? Why is quantity more important than quality? Love has never broke a heart, love has never made anyone cry. People broke many of hearts, people caused many of tears, yet they have the audacity to ask you to fight for them. Why, you didn't? I'm the same person I was when you climbed in that bed. Why am I so worthy now, and not then? How can I open my heart, when Im still hurting from the prior wounds you inflicted? No matter what I do to cover them up the pain is still there, it's a constant reminder that time doesn't heal all wounds, not when the cut is so deep it never stops bleeding.

Who I am

I'm going to tell you a secret...
I'm about to let you in on who I really am.
You ready?
Come close, I don't want you to miss a thing.
You ready, shhhhhh, that was one of those questions, that doesn't required an answer.
Okay, here goes, I'm about to get started.
Damn you about to hear some shit.
Something I never shared with anyone.
Now don't judge me after hearing this.
Whew, get prepared to hear the good, the bad, the ugly.
All right, here it is, listen at your own risk.
What I'm about to say is guaranteed to knock you off your feet?
Okay here goes the first day of the rest of my life.
I don't know were to start, so I'll start from the beginning.
Now like I said, it's going to come as a shock to you and stun a few, but this is who I am.
It was a big surprise to me that so many of you want to get to know the real me.
I feel special.
So now you'll know who I am and if you learnt anything here today you've learned that I'm a private person.
I share nothing about myself with anyone because that's just who I am.

Who are we?

Believe me when I tell you I never wanted us to end up this way.
I love you, just not like I loved you yesterday.
I really tried to hard to keep our family together, and build a happy home.
The more we're together, the more I feel alone.
Not once have you ever asked "what can I do for you".
Not once have you commented on the changes we're going through.
Yet I keep sacrificing my happiness and my need to live.
And all I think about is not hurting my kids.
I love our kids without a doubt.
And I don't want them to suffer because of my walking out.
The age difference played a big part.
You were totally different from what I'm use to, but you got inside my heart.
I thought I could change you, just like you thought you could change me.
Loving each other just wasn't easy.
So please don't make this any harder than it already is.
I will always respect you, you're the father of my kids.
Don't make me resent you for your unwillingness to let go.
We are not what we need, that I know.
Don't let pain consume your heart.
Get yourself together and get a new start.
But don't worry, we'll be there for our kids.

Our love that once was, is just not what it is.
I rehearsed in my mind what I was going to say to you.
Choosing my words carefully yet hating I have to choose.
I couldn't swallow being with someone and still be alone.
And if that be the case, I need to be on my own.
It was no us, just you and me.
No type of connection, so who are we?

Who's hurting me, is it you, or is it me.

You said it was a mistake that should of never happened, and I believed you.
You told me it was over and that, that would be the last time I'll be hurt by something that you do, and I believed that too.

Yet you keep saying I'm being paranoid each time you leave the house.
And if that I trusted and forgave you, what are the twenty- one questions about?

Why don't you understand why I'm feeling paranoid, when I'm around you and your phone rings you don't take your calls?
And if I ask you how your day went, it turns into an argument over issues not involved.

You think I'm picking each time I ask you a question, you make me feel insecure whenever we're around other women just by your actions.
You take everything I say to you directly to your heart.
And yet you're the one with your defense up and I'm the one torn apart.

Don't get me wrong, what you did hurt me real bad.

And sometimes I'm haunted by the memories, that often make me sad.
You act as if I should forget about all the bad times.
But how can I, when you're still constantly lying.
And yet I'm still being held hostage because of what you've done to me.
I'm afraid to turn my back on you because of your infidelities.

At times I feel like a burglar searching my own home, what's that all about?
Looking for clues of what you've done while me and the kids were out. Damn, why can't I just love and be loved and feel stress free?
Why can't I put myself first and stop putting you before me?

So if I'm being paranoid, you got me to this point.
Instead of coming to me, you went to someone else when I should have been the one giving you what you want.
So again who's hurting me, is it you or is it me?
I'll take some of the blame with that do you agree?

But if ever a time I needed strength, that time would be right now.
Because no mater how hard I try to forget about it the thought of it wears me down.
Now all this was sometimes ago but it's freshly on my mind. Stop forcing me to move on, healing has no time.

I do appreciate the fact that you're trying to do what's right.
Yet I can't stop these feelings I'm having, not even with all my might.
But who's hurting me, is it you or is t me?

Could it be we're both responsible for this tragedy?
There I go again putting you before me.
Taking the blame for something you created out of your stupidity.

You took everything that I held dear and close to me.

You stripped me of my self worth, along with my dignity.
You broke my heart, just to satisfy your lions.
You caused me to be afraid to love you and afraid to move on.

So who's hurting me, is it you or is it me ?

Who knew?

Who would of guessed we would end up here.
Loving each other so hard, that we can't see clear.
Damn, I loved you long before I knew what love was.
I wasn't in love with your money, I loved you, just because.
You were my best friend, I shared my secrets with you.
I shared my hopes and dreams and nightmares to.
I told you things no one else in this world knows.
You made it easy for me to carry a lighter load.
Then something happened, you started to change.
Everything was different our love, wasn't the same.
You began visiting and calling less.
I grew tired, and became restless.
I tried to be the glue, that held us together.
I truly thought we would be together forever.
I tried my damnest, not to break.
But how much pain did you think I could take.
Loving you was easy at first.
Then things changed, your love started to hurt.
You brought pain instead of joy.
And I took that as a sign you didn't love me know more.
I gave up because you gave up on me.
And believe me when I tell you, it wasn't easy.
How do you look at the one person constant in your life, and pretend that what you do is not about them.

When truthfully speaking, we go together like beginning and ending.
Where do we go when the roads has become so bumpy and hard to stay clear,
were do we go from here.
How can I look you in the face in show no sign of disgust?
When you single handily destroyed us.
You played and played to finally you blew.
Now you're asking me to trust you.
Who knew?

Who's behind those eyes?

I saw you yesterday even though I didn't know it was you.
I looked you right in your face and still didn't know who you were.
That look in your eyes alarmed me more than you know.
You looked at me as if you could see through me, you x-rayed me without a prescription, yet you hand me the bill.

Now you have the nerve to feel like I owe you, even though I still don't know who you are. Your eyes tell a story but leaves out the ending.
So how do you suppose I figure you out?

You committed thee unthinkable. You changed right before my eyes, as if you just committed some type of magic or as if I were hallucinating yet again.
Damn, it's the David Bland of the ghetto, trading in the cards for hearts, never realizing he made mine hurt. The only thing I can ever remembering disappearing is you. But, you always manage to reappear right back in some shit.
But it's cool. You don't know any better. I'm still trying to show you who's real in this relationship. But nah we won't take it there. A real player, never shows their hand.

If you treat gold like silver, which would be consider the higher value?
Things and people hold two different tittles, yet you have some Thinking, there one in the same.
Don't look at our relationship and compare it to something in your past.
And don't look at me and say," she don't mind" when you never asked a question.
I consider my love for you, untouchable.
So don't try and take from me, when you know I would give my life for my love which is one in the same.
I can't begin where you left off, because your beginning will never define my ending.
I can't give you less, and hope that you will increase the value. How could you?
When you already traded in it's real worth. And that was the part that held the highest value.
So, do you really think I can turn off and on when I'm in an off position?
Don't teach me anything different. The lesson is too expensive for me to afford,
why touch it.
Why try to entertain the thought, when you never give me answers to my questions, so I can move on.
You've changed me.
You taught me to fight you with whatever I can.
Now you want me to stop, because you can't take what you've been giving me for years.
Does that sound fair?
It doesn't feel it either.
It doesn't feel like it belongs to me.
I feel like a substitute for someone else and it's just affecting me more
I can relate to the feelings

I was there too.
Did you see me?
I was the one standing on the side looking lost, because I had no one to turn to.
I was the one with the tears running down her face?
Did you see me?
Yeah, that was me…
I was standing right over there.

Who's Family?

When I was growing up, family came first.
As I approached adulthood I learnt family is the worse.
Dealing with some family members make your enemies seems weak.
Nine times out of ten their liars, cheaters, and sneaks.
They don't give a damn how you feel.
All they care about is what you have to give.
They feed you false promises and empty dreams.
Then have the nerve to ask you, what does it all mean.
Why pretend to care, because we are blood.
That means nothing if you can't show me love.
Why must disagreements turn so physical?
Then after the aftermath you want to get all-biblical.
How can one be so wrong and think there so right.
Insinuating things that they think are true.
Going to others instead of coming to you.
Talking bout you like you don't exist.
With skeletons in their closets, ain't that a bitch!!

When it hurt so bad, and feels so good...

As I walk away from what seems like my whole life, I can't help but smile at all the memories. I was thinking back to the time you said let me get a little taste and that taste turned into a 4 hour love session. I also remember the time I was sitting on the back porch and you came up and began kissing me so passionately causing me to stand and stumble backward toward the wall. As I leaned in for a more deeper kiss your hands started to roam up and down my body causing me to flutter. I tried to push off but the kiss became more passionate. As I gripped u tighter I m becoming winded but aggressive at the same time. I began biting at your neck and ripping open your shirt placing soft kisses on your chest while roughly grinding into your manhood. You flipped the script back to you, because I was taken control and it was your show. I remember exactly how you did it. You pushed me back in to the wall while gripping my neck with one hand and snatching my panties off with the other, in one smooth motion. As you inserted your fingers inside my hot box I moan with pleasure, it sent a surge that made me quiver. I remembered how I began riding your fingers as I moved my body in circular motion. I'm smiling thinking about those soft kisses you were gently laying on my lips as your fist pounding my mound. As I open my eyes and part my lips I drop to my knees to catch the son or daughter that neither of us could afford. As your sweetness runs down my lips and chin, I ran my tongue across what remains. As I stand I can't help but look into your eyes and see the love before you spoke the words, and landed that forehead kiss. Wow the memories alone brings life back into this love affair that slowly faded. It's hard when it hurts so bad but feels so damn good.

Why do I need you to love me so bad?

Why am I so concern with what you need?
Your not even concern a little about me.
You keep pushing me away, and I keep fighting to stay.
I'm better than that, I don't want to be loved that way.
I don't want to have to fish, to see how you feel.
I'm better than that, I'm the real deal.
I have so much going for me and Im moving in the right direction.
And here I go, begging for your love and affection.
How can you not want a woman like me?
A woman that adds to your life not one that wants things for free.
I see now I can't help you close a circle that has a square.
Just like that don't fit, I can't force myself in there.
I can't make you love me, believe me I tried.
I gave you everything, I had inside.
I hope one day you find the person your truly looking for, but first build yourself up and learn to give just a little bit more.
Don't be so quick to push them out.
After all you're the one that don't know what love is all about.
You know what, I really wish you the best.
You had it but you couldn't see it past your mess.
You couldn't see how I was down for you?
You couldn't even see the bullshit you put me through.
I guess the saying is so very true.

You won't miss the water to the well runs dry, now that its dry what are you going to do.
I gave you all of me you gave me nothing, how sad.
Tell me again, why do I need you to love me so bad?